From
Pencils
to
Podcasts

Digital Tools for Transforming K–6 Literacy Practices

KATIE STOVER   LINDSAY YEARTA

Solution Tree | Press

a division of
Solution Tree

555 North Morton Street
Bloomington, IN 47404
800.733.6786 (toll free) / 812.336.7700
FAX: 812.336.7790

email: info@SolutionTree.com
SolutionTree.com

Visit go.SolutionTree.com/technology to download the free reproducibles in this book.

Printed in the United States of America

20 19 18 17 16   1 2 3 4 5

Library of Congress Cataloging-in-Publication Data

Names: Stover, Katie. | Yearta, Lindsay.
Title: From pencils to podcasts : digital tools for transforming K-6 literacy
    practices / authors: Katie Stover and Lindsay Yearta.
Description: Bloomington, IN : Solution Tree Press, 2016. | Includes
    bibliographical references and index.
Identifiers: LCCN 2016028122 | ISBN 9781942496274 (perfect bound)
Subjects: LCSH: Computers and literacy. | Language arts--Computer-assisted
    instruction.
Classification: LCC LC149.5 .S754 2016 | DDC 428.0078--dc23 LC record available at
https://lccn.loc.gov/2016028122

Solution Tree
Jeffrey C. Jones, CEO
Edmund M. Ackerman, President

Solution Tree Press
President: Douglas M. Rife
Senior Acquisitions Editor: Amy Rubenstein
Editorial Director: Tonya Maddox Cupp
Managing Production Editor: Caroline Weiss
Copy Editor: Ashante K. Thomas
Text and Cover Designer: Laura Cox
Intern: Laura Dzubay

For the next generation: Erin, Sean, Kaitlyn, and Kensley. —K. S.
For my Charles. Thank you for making it a wonderful world. —L. Y.

Acknowledgments

Whitney Becker
Third-Grade Teacher
Westview Elementary School
Spartanburg, South Carolina

Rebekah Clyborne
Third-Grade Teacher
Robert E. Cashion Elementary
Simpsonville, South Carolina

Anna Derrick
Third-Grade Teacher
Monarch Elementary School
Greenville, South Carolina

Victoria Ferguson
Second-Grade Teacher
Lone Oak Elementary School
Spartanburg, South Carolina

Brandy Gault
Fourth-Grade Teacher
Oakland Elementary School
Spartanburg, South Carolina

Alissa Goullet
Second-Grade Teacher
Welcome Elementary School
Greenville, South Carolina

Katharine Hale
Fifth-Grade Teacher
Abingdon Elementary School
Arlington, Virginia

Julie Jarriel
Reading Interventionist
High Point Academy
Denver, Colorado

Sarah McKinney
Kindergarten Teacher
Hunt Meadows Elementary School
Anderson, South Carolina

Jennifer Miller
Fifth-Grade Teacher
Old Pointe Elementary School
Rock Hill, South Carolina

Dawn Mitchell
Literacy Coach
Spartanburg County School District 6
Spartanburg, South Carolina

Claire Parman
Graduate Student in Communication
Sciences and Disorders
University of South Carolina
Columbia, South Carolina

McKinsey Payne
Sixth-Grade Teacher
Inman Intermediate School
Inman, South Carolina

Solution Tree Press would like to thank the following reviewers:

Connie Fink
Fifth-Grade Social Studies Teacher
University School of Nashville
Nashville, Tennessee

Heather Gauck
Special Education Resource Teacher
Harrison Park School
Grand Rapids, Michigan

Cindy Herren
Grades K–5 Technology Teacher
Brookview Elementary School
West Des Moines, Iowa

Joyce Jamerson
Literacy Coach and Reading Specialist
Gilbert, Arizona

Lisa Miller
Associate Professor of English
University of New Hampshire
Durham, New Hampshire

Melina Quon
Assistant Principal
Boulder Ridge Elementary School
Menifee, California

Christine Ruder
Third-Grade Teacher
Truman Elementary School
Rolla, Missouri

Denyell Suomi
First-Grade Teacher
Belgrade Central School
Belgrade, Maine

Visit **go.SolutionTree.com/technology** to download the free reproducibles in this book.

Table of Contents

Reproducible pages are in italics.

PART I
Tools to Facilitate Comprehension and Analysis

PART II
Tools to Facilitate Evaluation and Revision

PART III
Tools to Facilitate Performance and Publication

PART IV

Tools to Facilitate Assessment and Reflection

About the Authors

Katie Stover, PhD, is an assistant professor of education at Furman University in Greenville, South Carolina, where she teaches literacy methods for elementary learners, literacy assessment and instruction, and practicum with an emphasis on being a literacy interventionist and literacy coach. As a former elementary teacher and literacy coach, her research interests include teacher preparation and development in the area of literacy instruction and assessment. Additionally, Katie is interested in exploring how technology mediates literacy practices within and beyond the classroom setting. She continues to examine ways to engage diverse learners through culturally relevant practices that value all individuals while fostering compassionate global citizens who advocate for social justice and equality.

Katie presents at national, state, and regional conferences on topics ranging from reading and writing workshops to digital literacies and the use of diverse literature. She has consulted with large school districts and individual schools to tailor professional development to meet the needs of staff and students in the area of literacy.

Katie's publications include numerous book chapters and articles published in peer-reviewed journals including *The Reading Teacher, Literacy Research and Instruction, Journal of Digital Learning in Teacher Education,* and *Journal of Language and Literacy Education.* With Karen D. Wood and D. Bruce Taylor, she coauthored a book, *Smuggling Writing: Strategies That Get Students to Write Every Day in Every Content Area, Grades 3–12.*

Katie received a bachelor's degree in elementary education from the State University of New York at Cortland and her master's in reading education and doctorate in curriculum and instruction in urban literacy from the University of North Carolina at Charlotte.

To learn more about Katie's work, follow @KStover24 on Twitter.

 **Lindsay Yearta, PhD,** is an assistant professor of education at Winthrop University in Rock Hill, South Carolina, where she teaches courses in literacy and learning technologies. Lindsay has taught graduate and undergraduate courses and also has supervised student interns in classroom settings. She is a former elementary school teacher and continues to enjoy working closely with practicing prekindergarten through grade 12 teachers. Lindsay's research interests include digital literacies, critical literacy, and the use of digital tools to meet the needs of each student in the classroom.

Lindsay is a member of the International Literacy Association as well as the Technology in Literacy Education-Special Interest Group. She has received Teacher of the Year awards at both the preK–12 and higher education levels. Lindsay has presented at various U.S. conferences on topics that include using digital tools to increase student collaboration and communication, cultivating authentic learning experiences for all students, and creating a more inclusive classroom.

Lindsay's publications include book chapters as well as articles published in peer-reviewed journals such as *The Reading Teacher*, *Journal of Digital Learning in Teacher Education*, *Reading Horizons*, and *Journal of Language and Literacy Education*.

Lindsay earned her bachelor's degree in elementary education and her master's degree in reading education from Winthrop University. She earned her doctorate in curriculum and instruction in urban literacy from the University of North Carolina at Charlotte.

To learn more about Lindsay's work, follow @LYearta on Twitter.

To book Katie Stover or Lindsay Yearta for professional development, contact pd@SolutionTree.com.

INTRODUCTION

Literacy in the 21st Century

Humans have long used tools to create, construct, and evaluate. An artist uses spray paint to create a mural on the side of a building. A construction worker uses steel to build a skyscraper. A homeowner uses a level to ensure a painting is square. As teachers, we have the responsibility to equip our students with the tools that they need to fully participate in our interconnected, global society.

Why We Wrote This Book

To prepare students for the ever-expanding technological world, it is essential that we give them opportunities to use technology to augment traditional learning practices. The ability to communicate with wide audiences, create new products and innovations, and collaborate with people near and far is easier than ever. Smartphones, tablets, computers, and even interactive TV connect us now more than ever. Information is accessible at our fingertips from a range of sources.

In many of the classrooms we visit, we observe students using technology to conduct research work on projects and discuss their newfound knowledge. We see teachers using technology for assessment purposes. Allowing students to work in digital spaces enables them to communicate and collaborate with peers and a larger audience beyond the four walls of the classroom. Using technology as a tool is a part of our everyday lives. In fact, as coauthors living in different cities, we used Google Docs as a tool to draft, comment, revise, and complete this book.

Just before the 21st century, the International Reading Association (now the International Literacy Association) and the National Council of Teachers of English published new standards for English language arts (IRA & NCTE, 1996). These standards established that students should "use a variety of technological and information resources to gather and synthesize information and to create and communicate knowledge" (IRA & NCTE, 1996, p. 3). Yet, many teachers today lament a lack of familiarity and limited time to incorporate technology in the classroom (Stover, Kissel, Wood, & Putman, 2015). We believe that technology does not need to be an isolated activity that is tacked onto the instructional day; rather, it is an effective and efficient tool that can be integrated with preexisting lessons and instructional activities. We hope to provide teachers with a resource that offers practical suggestions to enhance teaching and learning by digitalizing familiar literacy practices such as reader response, reader's theater, research, and writing, to name a few. It is our aim to help teachers overcome perceived barriers and see the benefits of integrating technology meaningfully in classrooms with easy-to-implement digital tools.

Definitions of what it means to be literate shift constantly (Leu, 2000). Traditional notions of literacy that focused mainly on print-based reading and writing now include new literacies. The Internet and other information communication technologies (ICTs) result in evolving literacy practices for today's students (Lankshear & Knobel, 2006). For instance, using web 2.0 applications such as blogs and wikis fosters more active and transactional processes compared to web 1.0 tools including word-processing documents that involve mostly passive one-way delivery of information. According to the International Literacy Association's (2009) position statement on new technologies and reading instruction:

> To become fully literate in today's world, students must become proficient in the new literacies of 21st-century technologies. As a result, literacy educators have a responsibility to effectively integrate these new technologies into the curriculum, preparing students for the literacy future they deserve. (p. 1)

Students need to develop process-oriented skills rather than general content knowledge to be successful in the future workplace (Leu, Kinzer, Coiro, & Cammack, 2004). In these future roles, employees will need to process and critically analyze information, collaborate with others, and disseminate information using a range of modalities. ILA (2009) reminds us that students need to be Internet proficient to effectively participate in an era of global information sharing.

Students have greater access to technology both at home and in school. Yet there is a need for ongoing support for technology use beyond simple access. According to literacy experts Jay S. Blanchard and Alan E. Farstrup (2011), "Technology alone does not make the difference, but rather how it is used" (p. 303). Researchers Douglas Kellner and Jeff Share (2007) note that providing access to technology does not guarantee that it will be used "for meaningful instructional tasks" (p. 306). In fact, the teacher is one of the most significant factors associated with effective technology integration (Mandell, Sorge, & Russell, 2002). ILA (2009) reminds us that educators have a responsibility to integrate technologies into the curriculum to better prepare students. Blanchard and Farstrup (2011) assert, "Teachers must be at the heart of the decision-making and instructional-planning process as technologies are introduced and implemented" (p. 305). Thus, enhancing teachers' knowledge of tools, pedagogy for instructional use, and providing necessary support to address educational goals and standards should be considered (Larkin & Finger, 2011; Perkins & Saltsman, 2010). With these aims and responsibilities in mind, it is our goal to provide educators with authentic strategies to seamlessly embed technology into the existing curriculum.

Although we live in a world surrounded by technology, it is essential that teachers incorporate technology in purposeful ways to enhance students' learning experiences. Elizabeth Dobler (2011/2012) states that "the tool must let us do something better—more efficiently, more effectively—than we can without the technology" (p. 18). Rather than being isolated tools that replace the teacher, technologies should be fully integrated to foster student-centered learning with the goals of promoting lifelong reading habits and reading achievement (Blanchard & Farstrup, 2011). Technology enhances curricular integration and supports specific learning goals (Northrop & Killeen, 2013). In order to be effective, technology integration should be routine and support curriculum goals (Edutopia, 2008). According to Blanchard and Farstrup (2011), "Technology provides indispensable resources used as part of an extensive range of new and traditional instructional tools geared to the needs of children" (p. 294). In this book, we suggest ways to facilitate students' abilities to create, communicate, collaborate, share, and assess learning using a range of technology tools.

Digital tools can enhance instruction and learning for students. *From Pencils to Podcasts: Digital Tools for Transforming K–6 Literacy Practices* discusses and demonstrates how technology use can foster skill development and deeper thinking through authentic reading, writing, and communication practices in the classroom and beyond. The digital tools we present throughout this book can be used to mediate a variety of literacy practices to enhance students' oral language, fluency, comprehension, and writing abilities. Students simultaneously develop essential skills to foster communication, collaboration, and sharing with authentic audiences via technology. Digital tools allow students to create, communicate, collaborate, and share within and beyond the four walls of the classroom in new and innovative ways.

How This Book Is Organized

We envision this book as a toolbox filled with strategies and suggestions to help improve classroom instruction while integrating technology. You can read it as a resource by locating a particular tool to meet your students' instructional needs or by exploring digital tools you are interested in trying. In this way, you can see examples of how other teachers used the tools and read the step-by-step instructions for implementing the technology in your own classroom. Each chapter provides sample tools and strategies that we have found to be successful in fostering digital literacy practices with grades K–6 learners. We do not believe in one-size-fits-all approaches and therefore offer these as possibilities.

The chapters are grouped into the following four parts.

    I.   Tools to Facilitate Comprehension and Analysis
   II.   Tools to Facilitate Evaluation and Revision
  III.   Tools to Facilitate Performance and Publication
  IV.   Tools to Facilitate Assessment and Reflection

Each chapter presents a unique digital tool to mediate literacy practices, beginning with a vignette, followed by a section grounded in research and a description of the suggested digital tool. We then describe how to implement the digital tool in the classroom and offer a classroom example to give the reader a comprehensive understanding of the tool and its role in facilitating literacy teaching and learning. Each chapter concludes with suggestions for integration in the content areas as well as adaptations to provide the reader with multiple ways to consider integrating technology tools in the classroom. These suggestions are not exclusive but rather are meant to offer possibilities.

Web 2.0 technology allows users to create content on the Internet, making it easier to share with a wider audience. As Jason Ohler (2005/2006) notes, "Media-based [content] are now everyone's to create [and] everyone's to watch and enjoy" (p. 44). Digital creation of information allows students to become active creators rather than passive consumers of multimedia (Ohler, 2005/2006). Part I houses the tools that facilitate comprehension and analysis. In chapter 1 we describe the use of digital word walls and tools such as wikis, digital images, and online dictionaries to enhance students' vocabularies—specifically their knowledge of Greek and Latin roots. Chapter 2 details how a fifth-grade teacher used the Edmodo online platform to foster communication between elementary and college students about shared literature.

Although writing is a communicative process, traditional literacies using paper and pencils limit students' opportunities to communicate to wider audiences beyond the classroom (Merchant, 2005). However, new technologies have broadened the role of communication and mediate social practices. According to the International Society for Technology in Education, students need opportunities to "communicate information and ideas effectively to multiple audiences using a variety of media and formats" (ISTE, 2007). In chapter 3 we share how students used Kidblog to participate in online book clubs. Part II moves to tools that facilitate evaluation and revision. Chapter 4 presents ways to engage students in research using multimedia sources. Chapter 5 details how to foster a wide community of readers through the creation and sharing of book reviews via audioBoom, QR codes, and Twitter.

Web 2.0 tools promote collaboration among Internet users (Laru, Naykki, & Jarvela, 2012) and can have a profound effect on learning and thinking (Solomon & Schrum, 2007). Working together to co-construct knowledge can enhance the depth and breadth of students' understanding (Coiro, Castek, & Guzniczak, 2011), foster discussion, enhance literacy learning and communication skills, and support a sense of community (Larson, 2009).

The need to evaluate online content is increasingly important in our digital world. Chapter 6 describes how to use Google Drive to facilitate online revision circles as students collaboratively write and revise a reader's theatre script. Chapter 7 provides an approach to reader's theater that incorporates digital tools such as iMovie and YouTube to improve students' fluency and enhance students' self-evaluation and sharing with a wider audience.

A major aspect of web 2.0 applications is the ability for users to interact and share their collective intelligence (O'Reilly, 2005). Students can easily share about themselves and about books they are reading, and publish their own writing. As Katie Stover and Chase Young (2014) posit, "Writing in the 21st century classroom has shifted from a single author writing for the teacher as the audience to collaborative writing for authentic audiences within and beyond the four walls of the classroom" (p. 185). Part III presents tools that facilitate performance and publication. Chapter 8 explores how a fourth-grade class used digital tools, such as Piktochart and Easel.ly, to create infographics and improve their informational writing skills. In chapter 9 we share how kindergarten students used the Puppet Pals app to engage in collaborative digital storytelling. Chapter 10 describes digital tools like Book Creator that facilitate publishing student writing to share with a wide audience. Allowing students to publish in digital spaces allows them to write for a more authentic audience and provides them the opportunity to elicit and obtain feedback from a variety of readers.

Part IV includes chapters 11 through 14, which focus on the use of digital tools to promote authentic assessment and reflection of student learning. According to the International Literacy Association (2009), formative assessment is not about grades but instead a natural aspect of teaching and learning on a daily basis. Formative assessment is purposeful and supports continued growth. The way assessment works in new literacy spaces has significant implications for how teachers approach literacy instruction in classrooms.

Chapter 11 presents how students develop as readers by using a digital time line to create and share their reading histories. Allowing students to publish in a digital space highlights that they can write for a more authentic audience and provides them with the opportunity to elicit and obtain feedback from a variety of readers. In chapter 12, we describe how using the app Confer (soon to be split into two tools, the other called Snapfolio) to digitalize anecdotal notes for individual students makes the collection, organization, and analysis of student data more efficient and effective. Chapter 13 discusses how writers can reflect upon and share their writing with an authentic audience through digital portfolios such as Seesaw. Digital portfolios also offer a platform for teachers to assess students' writing to then adjust their teaching practices accordingly. Chapter 14 highlights the use of Lino, an online canvas, as an informal assessment of students' reading comprehension. Students can record their thinking before, during, and after reading to improve comprehension and provide their teacher with a window into their thinking. (Visit **go.Solution Tree.com/technology** to access material related to this book.)

Throughout the book, you'll see QR codes like the one in the margin. QR codes are square machine-readable codes that can be found on a variety of documents, from advertising flyers to everyday products at the grocery store. QR codes give the user instant access to information on the web. When the user scans the QR code using the built-in camera on a tablet or smartphone, he or she is taken to a linked website. Users have instant access to digital text and resources without the need for paper and pencils or typing in long website addresses. Users can download free apps to scan QR codes such as Kaywa Reader and QR Reader for their smartphones and tablets. To create a QR code, simply go to a QR-code-generating website, such as QR Stuff or QR Code Generator, and paste a hyperlink into the URL box. The website will then generate a free QR code that users can copy and paste into a document or a website of their own.

Technology, when used intentionally, enhances teaching and learning as students have more opportunities to create, collaborate, communicate, and share. It also provides teachers with opportunities for authentic assessment of student understanding and progress. This book offers a plethora of digital tools and instructional strategies from our own teaching experiences, from the classrooms of teachers we work closely with, and from representative classrooms composed of experiences gathered from our extensive time spent in a range of classrooms. We hope you find these digital tools and instructional strategies useful in your own classroom.

PART I

Tools to Facilitate
Comprehension and Analysis

Digital Word Wall

As the students transition from mathematics to the beginning of the language arts block, they know it is time for vocabulary study. They pull out their homework from the previous night, a traditional exercise of writing ten words with their accompanying definitions.

"Vocabulary is boring," Rianya mumbles from her seat.

"I said that to my mom and she told me that she used to write definitions for homework when she was in school, too," Jarvis replies.

Mr. Lowry hears the comments as he walks around the room. He isn't happy with his vocabulary instruction either, but he doesn't want to cut it altogether. He has about ten to twenty minutes a day to teach vocabulary, just enough time for him to check the students' vocabulary homework and go over a few definitions. He knows vocabulary is essential in improving students' comprehension and overall intelligence, but he does not know how to squeeze quality instruction into the tiny time frame the schedule allows.

Having a large vocabulary is beneficial for students (Mixan, 2013), as vocabulary knowledge is closely connected to comprehension and overall intelligence (Anderson & Freebody, 1981; Cunningham & Stanovich, 1997). Additionally, vocabulary instruction has been identified as one of the five most essential components of literacy instruction (National Institute of Child Health and Human Development, 2000).

But like Mr. Lowry, many teachers are frustrated trying to find ways to provide high-quality, engaging vocabulary instruction in a limited time period. Due to time constraints and an overabundance of content standards to cover, vocabulary instruction is often neglected. This exacerbates the problem of the *vocabulary gap*, or the gap that occurs when students come to school with differing vocabularies (Biemiller & Boote, 2006). Left alone, the vocabulary gap will continue to widen between proficient and struggling readers (Graves, 2009; Hart & Risley, 1995), which can impact students' success in reading (Beck, McKeown, & Kucan, 2002; Biemiller, 2001; Hart & Risley, 1995) as well as their overall success in school.

In order for vocabulary instruction to be most effective, teachers should ensure that students are able to experience direct, explicit instruction; actively engage in vocabulary study; and develop a sense of word consciousness (Graves & Watts-Taffe, 2002; Manyak et al., 2014; Taylor, Mraz, Nichols, Rickelman, & Wood, 2009). While direct instruction and word consciousness are certainly vital components of vocabulary instruction, this chapter deals mainly with promoting students' active engagement in vocabulary study.

This chapter will show you how to incorporate digital tools in vocabulary instruction, helping students to build essential skills in fun, engaging ways.

Learn the Benefits of Digital Tools for Vocabulary Instruction

One way to promote active engagement of vocabulary in the classroom is the interactive word wall (Harmon, Wood, & Kiser, 2009). Students make connections between words and meanings, engage in repeated experiences with the words, and exercise a degree of choice in the vocabulary study (Harmon et al., 2009). Once a teacher decides to implement an interactive word wall in the classroom, the next step is to decide on a topical focus. What words should students study in an interactive manner?

Deciding on which words should be taught is a daunting task. The English language has more words than any other (Zutell, 2008), and to teach each word individually would not be time efficient. Instead, the best approach to vocabulary instruction may be a morphological one, an approach that teaches word parts (Baumann et al., 2002; Taylor et al., 2009). This approach is an efficient, effective one because knowledge of a few word parts provides students access to understanding a myriad of vocabulary words (Baumann et al., 2002; Taylor et al., 2009). Specifically, studying Greek and Latin roots is an integral part of any comprehensive vocabulary program (Rasinski, Padak, Newton, & Newton, 2011). Students can ascertain many word meanings with the knowledge of one Greek or Latin root. Timothy V. Rasinski, Nancy Padak, Joanna Newton, and Evangeline Newton (2011) provide the example of knowing that *trac* and *tract* "mean to pull, draw or drag" and this can help students understand words like "*track, tractor, traction, retract, detract, abstract, contract, contraction, extract, intractable, protractor, subtract, trace, retrace*" as well as many others (p. 134).

How do we best combine an interactive word wall with the study of Greek and Latin roots? Why, we go digital, of course! Let's examine the benefits of incorporating digital tools in vocabulary instruction and look at some easy-to-use wikis to create a digital word wall as an interactive space to foster vocabulary study.

Encouraging students to engage in digital word study has several benefits, such as students finding the digital word wall a faster, simpler, and more motivating method to learn vocabulary (Yearta, 2012). Additionally, using digital tools gives students access to more words, allowing them to make additional connections and develop a deeper understanding of Greek and Latin roots. Of course, another benefit to using a digital word wall as opposed to a traditional word wall is that students can more easily save their work, as is the case with many digital tools. There are no loose papers to keep track of and organize; rather, there is a central location for students to save their work and for teachers to assess it. Also, digital word walls created as wikis can be accessed from anywhere as long as students have an Internet connection. This means that students can create and collaborate across great distances.

Access Tools for Digital Word Study

Students can use several online tools when they are creating digital word walls (Yearta & Wash, 2015). One option for digital word study is for teachers to use a classroom wiki. Table 1.1 lists five sites that provide free, safe spaces for teachers and students to collaborate online. While these tools share many of the same advantages, this chapter describes how to use PBworks EDUHub as a digital tool for word study.

Table 1.1: Digital Tools for Vocabulary Study

Tool and URL	QR Code	Description
Wikispaces www.wikispaces.com/content/classroom		Wikispaces provides a collaborative, safe, free space for students and teachers to learn together. This site allows teachers to see what their students are doing in real time. Therefore, they are able to provide immediate feedback. The teacher can assign projects to teams and can create templates to help students get started.
PBworks EDUHub www.pbworks.com/education		PBworks EDUHub provides teachers with free wikis. Once the teacher has created the wiki, he or she can create student accounts without needing student email addresses. Files are easily accessible by phone, tablet, and computer.
Word Central www.wordcentral.com		Powered by Merriam-Webster, Word Central provides a student-friendly online dictionary, spaces for students to build their own dictionaries, and games to test vocabulary knowledge and build skills. A special section for educators provides additional resources for word study.

continued ➡

Merriam-Webster www.merriam-webster.com		Merriam-Webster gives users access to its online dictionary, thesaurus, Spanish dictionary, medical dictionary, and learner's dictionary. The site also helps students build vocabulary with its featured word of the day, games, and videos.
Wordsmyth www.wordsmyth.net		Wordsmyth contains three levels of dictionaries (beginner, intermediate, and advanced) as well as specialized and illustrated dictionaries geared toward school-age users. A variety of search tools, games, and instructional support resources make this site very user-friendly for students and educators.

Using a wiki to study vocabulary allows for increased collaboration. Additionally, it enables access to several other digital tools, such as online dictionaries, to determine word meanings. Instead of searching through pages of a traditional dictionary to find the word, students can simply type the word into a search engine. Using an online dictionary is more efficient and also beneficial for students who struggle with sound-symbol relationships and have difficulty with locating words in a traditional dictionary. If students are attempting to gather and investigate a variety of words that contain a specific Greek or Latin root, they can use websites to locate the words. For example, if the target root is *derm*, students could visit https://msu.edu/~defores1/gre/roots/gre_rts_afx2.htm or https://en.wikipedia.org/wiki/List_of_Greek_and_Latin_roots_in_English to locate and explore words that contain the root *derm*, such as *pachyderm* or *epidermis*.

When using a traditional dictionary, the words that students find typically contain the Greek or Latin root as a prefix. For example, with *derm* students might only find the example of *dermatology*. This is due to the alphabetic layout of a traditional dictionary. Students can then use a digital dictionary such as Word Central (www.wordcentral.com) to continue the research on various words. By allowing students to use the Internet to investigate words that contain the Greek or Latin root embedded within the word, vocabulary study can become more robust.

Incorporating digital tools like those listed here offers clear benefits for vocabulary teaching and learning. But how can teachers make the leap from delivering nondigital instruction to preparing instruction that uses technology meaningfully? Let's look at how teachers can use the popular wiki PBworks to make this transition.

Transition to Digital Word Study Using PBworks EDUHub

Initiate digital word study in the classroom by first familiarizing students with the traditional version of the modified Frayer model (Yearta, 2012) before they begin creating the digital representations of word study. An advantage of having paper copies is that the students can continue with their word study even in the face of technological issues. The modified Frayer model has five components. (See figure 1.1 for a sample student assignment using the modified Frayer model.)

1. **Root:** Students list the Greek or Latin root under study in the center of the model
2. **Meaning:** Students write the meaning of the root in the top left box
3. **Example:** Students provide an example of a word containing the root in the top right box
4. **Definition:** Students include the definition of the example in the bottom right box
5. **Illustration and sentence:** Students note an illustration and sentence containing the example word in the bottom left box

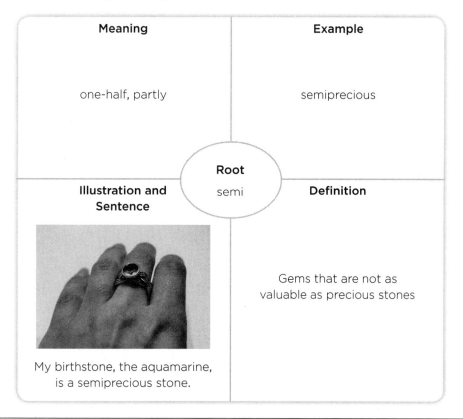

Figure 1.1: A modified Frayer model for the root *semi*.

To begin the move to the digital landscape for word study, go to www.pbworks.com and click the Get Started button. Then, choose the EDUHub option. The basic edition is free and will be adequate for most classroom teachers. PBworks then asks that you choose a URL address, guarantee that you are not using the site for commercial purposes, and provide an email address and password.

At this point, there are a multitude of options to customize the digital word wall to meet students' specific needs. For example, you might establish one word wall for the entire class, or you might divide the class into groups and each group can have its own word wall. To give each group its own word wall, list students' group names or numbers and link each to a new page. The student can select his or her group number to access the group's digital word wall from the wiki home screen.

Next, create a chart with the roots that students will be focusing on for the week. (See figure 1.2 for a sample.) Michael F. Graves (2009) suggests that students study two to four new root words per week. Link each root to a new page that students will then use to share their modified Frayer models (Yearta, 2012).

Week 1	co— together inter— between/among mis— wrong/bad
Week 2	semi— one-half/partly terra— earth port— carry
Week 3	audi— to hear dict— to say/speak meter— measure

Figure 1.2: Linked roots.

When the student clicks on one of the roots for the particular week, he or she is taken to the group's page with all modified Frayer models for that particular root. For example, let's say a student, Charlie, clicks on *co*. He will be taken to the *co* page and will construct a modified Frayer model for *co* by clicking on the Edit tab and choosing Table. He can then insert a table to use for his modified Frayer model (figure 1.3, page 15).

Students quickly become familiar with the wiki features and often learn shortcuts with increased practice and interaction with the digital tool. Students can work on their modified Frayer models from home, school, or anywhere with an Internet connection.

In the section Observe Digital Word Wall Tools in Action, we check back in with Mr. Lowry and his class to see how using digital tools to create word walls improved their vocabulary teaching and learning.

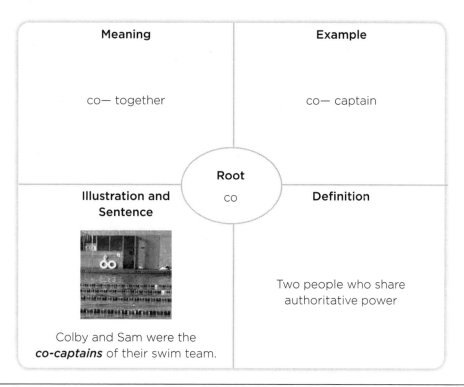

Figure 1.3: Screenshot of a modified Frayer model for *co*.

Observe Digital Word Wall Tools in Action

After Mr. Lowry is finished introducing the digital word wall to his students, they use their school-provided laptops to log in to the class PBworks wiki. As soon as students access their group page, Mr. Lowry directs their attention to the Promethean whiteboard so that he can demonstrate how to create a table. He also reminds students of the modified Frayer model's components and reviews several examples. After viewing an example for the root *co*, each group works on creating its own modified Frayer model for *co*. Working on the same root allows students to focus on becoming familiar with the wiki as well as using digital dictionaries and searching for digital images.

To provide students with some choice in tools, Mr. Lowry demonstrates several online dictionaries for the students to use. He starts with Word Central. He also shows them how to look up words on Merriam-Webster's site. The last digital dictionary that Mr. Lowry shares with his students is Wordsmyth. It allows users to choose from three leveled dictionaries: beginner, intermediate, and advanced. Depending on the age and ability level of the students, any number of digital dictionaries can be used. Essentially, the salient features are that students can input the word and have instantaneous access to the word's meaning. An additional positive feature of a digital dictionary is that students have other options at their fingertips. In other words, if the student does not understand the definition provided by one site, he or she can explore a different digital dictionary.

Teaching students which images they are allowed or not allowed to use can be complicated, but Google makes it a bit more straightforward. Mr. Lowry decides to show students how to use the search tools in Google in order to help them select images with the proper licenses. Mr. Lowry has his students conduct a Google search for the image that they want. Then, he has students select Search Tools, which will appear under the search bar. Next, his students click on Usage Rights and select Labeled for Reuse or Labeled for Noncommercial Reuse. When using this method, several images appear. After clicking on an image, students see a larger thumbnail and the image's title. Mr. Lowry then advises his students to visit the page in order to confirm the image's license. Mr. Lowry has his students provide the URL and the author's name within the modified Frayer model even if the images are free for commercial use with no attribution required.

After students create at least one modified Frayer model on the digital word wall, Mr. Lowry displays several student-created samples on the Promethean whiteboard and leads the class in collaborative group discussions. This allows the groups to engage in conversations about the process of working on the digital word wall as well as talk about the completed modified Frayer models. With the added benefit of technology, access to digital dictionaries, and a plethora of images, vocabulary study has become more interesting for the students. Instead of memorizing their list of ten words for the test, only to forget the meanings as soon as the test is complete, students engage in active, collaborative vocabulary study, which leads to a deeper, more complex understanding of the vocabulary words and word parts. In fact, Mr. Lowry notices that when his students come across unknown words in their content area reading, they use their knowledge of Greek and Latin roots to understand the unknown words. For example, when Brandon reads about an aqueduct, he determines that it has something to do with water because he remembers that *aqua* is a Latin root meaning *water*. Seeing his students use their newfound knowledge in this way helps Mr. Lowry realize that the students are taking this deeper understanding of vocabulary and making connections across content areas.

Understand Content Area Connections and Extended Applications

As students read in the content areas, they encounter new words, new concepts, and new meanings for words (Blachowicz & Fisher, 2006). Fortunately, the digital word wall is highly adaptable and students can create a content area digital word wall. Once they become familiar with the wiki, they can add pages for other content areas. For example, students could study words or concepts related to World War II.

Julie Jackson and Rose Narvaez (2013) studied the effects of a science-content interactive word wall. Teachers looked at the conceptual relationships between words and sketched out a graphic organizer of how the concepts were related. They put these large visual scaffolds on the classroom walls and invited students to add drawings and objects to illustrate the scientific concepts. Jackson and Narvaez (2013) found that the word walls were "useful to students not only in unifying related terms and concepts, but also in helping students visualize connections between vocabulary inquiry experiments, their own interests, and experience" (p. 49). Teachers can digitize the content area word wall by allowing students to visualize their own connections between and among concepts in a digital space such as a wiki. For example, when studying abiotic (nonliving) and biotic (living) factors, students could create a modified Frayer model for each type of factor. With some simple changes to the modified Frayer model, students could create and place the graphic organizer in figure 1.4 on a digital word wall.

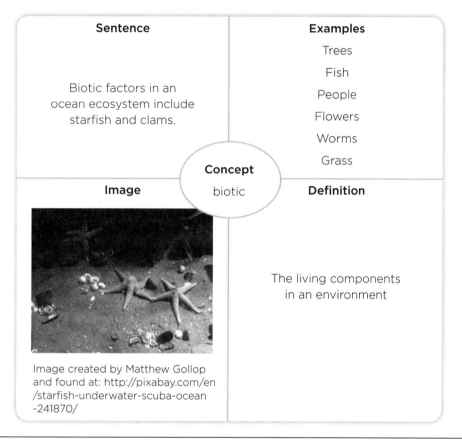

Figure 1.4: A modified Frayer model for *biotic*.

Make Adaptations

English learners (ELs), especially native Spanish speakers, benefit from Greek and Latin root instruction due to the prevalence of Greek- and Latin-based words in the Spanish language (Blachowicz & Fisher, 2006; Rasinski et al., 2011). To initiate vocabulary study, teachers should choose words that have common roots in both the native and English languages (Blachowicz & Fisher, 2006).

An additional adaptation is the vocabulary self-selection strategy (Haggard, 1986). Janis M. Harmon, Karen D. Wood, Wanda B. Hedrick, and Michelle Gress (2008) find the vocabulary self-selection strategy to be an effective approach to meeting struggling readers' needs. Teachers can have students self-select the words from content areas that students find to be personally challenging to study. This is a way to differentiate vocabulary instruction. While a common concern might be that students will select words that are familiar, research suggests that students do, in fact, choose words that are challenging. In their study of middle school students, Harmon and colleagues (2008) find that the struggling readers are able to choose the words for study that are "necessary for understanding the passage" (p. 45). To encourage additional experience with these cognitively challenging words, students can then create modified Frayer models for each self-selected word in an effort to further study and better understand their meanings.

Digital Reader Response

Fifth grader Jamilet is excited to use Edmodo to talk to her reading buddy. However, when she realizes that their communication will be through written posts on the website, she becomes discouraged. Jamilet rarely posts and therefore demonstrates minimal comprehension of the book her class is discussing on Edmodo. Thinking that her communication with Jamilet could have been overwhelming, her reading buddy, Rebekah, a college student studying to become a teacher, attempts to nudge Jamilet by simplifying the comments and questions she posed on Edmodo. Yet, even this approach does not seem to encourage deeper posts from Jamilet. Knowing that Jamilet struggles with both comprehension and written expression, her teacher, Ms. Hale, suggests that Rebekah try a different method of teaching Jamilet how to respond to text. Rebekah agrees with Ms. Hale and decides to post a video on Edmodo to demonstrate her own reader response on Jamilet's wall. In the video, Rebekah models how to read, think aloud about what happened in the text, and summarize the events on a sticky note through drawing and writing. She draws a picture on a sticky note and shows Jamilet how to stick it directly on the page she just read.

After watching Rebekah's video, Jamilet is inspired to do the same and even posts her own video of her reader response for Rebekah. Jamilet enjoys the process of using sticky notes to respond to text and she feels like she understands more of what she read. Reading and processing written posts on Edmodo overwhelmed Jamilet, but the use of multimodalities, such as viewing and creating videos, seems to be the key to her success.

Sometimes, students like Jamilet need information presented in different ways. In this chapter, we'll explore how the multimodal tool Edmodo can accommodate multiple learning styles and support the development of students' reader-response and communication skills.

Learn the Benefits of Digital Tools for Interacting With Text and Others

When readers respond to text, whether orally or in writing, they create their own meaning based on personal experiences and prior knowledge (Rosenblatt, 1978). Reader-response theory suggests that "each reader breathes life into the text" (Larson, 2009, p. 638). Rapidly changing ICTs cause constant shifts in the way we interact with and respond to text (ILA, 2001; Leu, 2002). As a result, teachers have a responsibility to engage learners in meaningful technology use (ILA, 2009). According to the ISTE (2008) standards, teachers need to help students "communicate relevant information and ideas effectively . . . using a variety of digital age media and formats." The teacher's role has shifted from leading discussions and transmitting information to facilitating discussion and positioning students as active contributors to conversations.

Technology provides students with an online space to participate in interactive, asynchronous conversations outside of time constraints. Using these forums for online literature discussions, students share their thoughts and voice their opinions about books in a socially constructed learning environment. Participants communicate without interruption and have equal opportunities to contribute using asynchronous message boards (Grisham & Wolsey, 2006). Katie Stover, Lindsay Yearta, and Caroline Harris (2016) find that online literature discussions provide students with additional think-time to construct responses. As Dana L. Grisham and Thomas D. Wolsey (2006) note, "Asynchronous communications are interactive, like discussions, but thoughtful, like written discourse" (p. 652).

Writing is a communicative process that serves many functions (Graham & Harris, 2013). When used in online spaces to respond to literature, writing helps students become facilitators of discussion that extends beyond the classroom into virtual learning spaces (Larson, 2009). Several studies indicate that online literature discussions have the potential to strengthen communication skills and build a sense of community (Carico & Logan, 2004; Grisham & Wolsey, 2006; Larson, 2009; Wolsey, 2004). Lotta C. Larson (2009) finds that students respond deeply to the literature, share their ideas, and consider multiple perspectives when they engage in online book discussions. In these ways, multimodal digital tools help teachers to deepen student comprehension as they engage in book discussions with a variety of audiences beyond the classroom.

Access Tools to Engage Students in Digital Book Discussions

Edmodo, Scribble Press, and Educreations are digital tools that support students' reader responses using multimodalities (see table 2.1, page 21). This chapter focuses on the social networking tool Edmodo. Teachers can easily use Edmodo to foster communication among students. Using an invitation-only approach, teachers create a free account and request students to join using a unique code. Parents may also be granted access to this code as a way to monitor their child's work. Once all students (and parents, if invited) have joined the group, the code is deactivated. Using this secure online space, students can communicate safely to share ideas, solve problems, and discuss various concepts they are learning in class. In this way, teachers and students can communicate in real time.

Table 2.1: Digital Tools for Multimodal Conversations About Reading

Tool and URL	QR Code	Description
Edmodo www.edmodo.com		Edmodo provides a safe space for online communication and collaboration. Teachers and students can access blended learning spaces and online resources, and parents can review their child's work.
Scribble Press app http://app.scribblepress.com		This free app features hundreds of drawing tools, digital stickers, and templates to enable users to write and illustrate notes, pages, or storybooks online. A special section for teachers provides examples of ways to use the app in the classroom. The paid upgrade to the premium version permits users to record narration, select from music tracks, and choose additional stickers, templates, and drawing tools.
Educreations https://www.educreations.com		Educreations records voice, drawing, and inserted images to produce a video presentation that can easily be shared online.

To differentiate content and activities for students based on their ability levels, teachers can create small groups within the online class. One way to do this is through book clubs that group students based on interest and independent reading levels. Within their groups, students can begin a new threaded discussion by creating a new note to display on their group's page, and they can respond easily to their peers' posts by replying directly underneath the peers' posts. Edmodo also allows users to react using emojis such as smiley faces to indicate outstanding work. Using emoticons gives users yet another way to convey information in online environments (Grisham & Wolsey, 2006; Leu et al., 2004).

Transition to Multimodal Reader Responses Using Edmodo

When introducing students to Edmodo, it is helpful to display the website and demonstrate how to create an account and log in to the website using the group access code. Next, give students a virtual tour to introduce basic features such as how to access small groups, how to post, and how to reply. Eventually, students can explore the settings to update their profiles with photos or avatars to represent their identities. Once teachers create accounts and add students to groups, students are ready to engage in online conversations with their peers. Teachers can provide anyone with the access code in order to join the group. Participants may include parents, students from other schools, or college students studying to become teachers.

The goal is to encourage a lively and thoughtful conversation through digital response. In order to reach this goal, modeling expectations regarding quantity and quality of responses is helpful. For example, teachers might create a checklist with criteria for online conversations and post it near the computers or as a digital table in Edmodo as a constant reminder (see figure 2.1). Additionally, creating and implementing a schedule for students to respond regularly can usefully frame expectations for the minimum frequency of responses. In particular, for classrooms with limited access to technology, a rotational computer schedule allows all students to have opportunities to participate. Certainly, students are not limited to these times, as they can log in during free time and from home.

Remember to . . .

- [ ] Acknowledge your partner's contribution to the discussion.
- [ ] Politely agree or disagree.
- [ ] Support your claim with evidence from the text.
- [ ] Use complete sentences to convey your thoughts.
- [ ] Be respectful; use appropriate language and follow online etiquette.

Figure 2.1: Checklist for online conversations.

For students who face challenges with getting started, open-ended prompts such as "Have you ever . . ." or "What do you think . . ." can be used to help them engage in conversations. Larson (2009) shares numerous ways to engage students in digital reader response, including aesthetic or emotional responses, cognitive responses to infer and predict, interpretive responses to examine moral and theme, and clarification responses when confused about the text or material. With ongoing practice and scaffolding, students will eventually begin to independently initiate and compose thoughtful responses to the literature and to their peers.

In the section Observe Multimodal Reader-Response Tools in Action, we check in with Jamilet and other students in Ms. Hale's fifth-grade class to see how they and their reading mentors use digital tools to respond to texts and discuss them with each other.

Observe Multimodal Reader-Response Tools in Action

Fifth graders in Ms. Hale's class participate in reading partnerships based on their independent reading levels. Ms. Hale groups her fifth graders based on similar reading abilities and each group selects a book of interest to discuss during class. Each student group is also paired with a reading mentor who reads the same text and communicates digitally using Edmodo. The reading mentors, studying to become teachers, teach their fifth-grade mentees reading strategies and encourage them to apply them to their own reading. These experiences excite the fifth graders and allow them to have authentic conversations about their reading while receiving personalized literacy instruction. While this partnership involves preservice teachers as reading mentors, teachers can create heterogeneous groupings where students with higher levels of mastery partner with peers from their own class or another classroom across the globe.

Students develop as readers through the ongoing digital conversations. One group demonstrates its abilities to make connections and inferences related to the main character. This is evident when Jada begins to comment about the main character, Donovan. She states, "It seems to me that Donovan makes a lot of bad choices. Like escaping out the window before his detention was over." After noticing similar comments in her peers' posts, Claire, the group's reading mentor, uses this common thread as a springboard for her post. She asks the students to consider a specific quality of the main character, Donovan (see figure 2.2).

Claire said   *Sept. 18*

In the first couple of chapters we see that Donovan is a real troublemaker. He ends up in detention, gets in trouble with teachers, and worst of all is his big accident with the Atlas statue. However, there are a couple of details I noticed that I think might indicate something deeper about Donovan and his character. For example, on pg. 3 Donovan tells us, "There is no logical explanation for what I did. It had to come from my DNA. That's why I needed ancestry.com." What do you think this tells us about Donovan? Have you ever done something that you can't explain?

Jada said   *Sept. 22*

I think that when Donavan said "it had to come from my DNA, he might have meant that he could not explain what happened. But I have a feeling that when Donavan finds out where he belongs he may start to be a good kid.

Jada said   *Sept. 22*

Something I did that I could not explain was about a year ago a yelled at my twin sister and all of a sudden I kicked her right in the face, felt so bad I did not know what to say to my parents.

Nardos said   *Sept. 22*

Donavon is a good kid, he just doesn't know it yet! Sometimes I do things that I don't know why I did. Once I picked a fight with my sister for no apparent reason. This tells me that Donavon is an ordinary kid inside (not a trouble maker)!—I love the book so far! I think that it's interesting and full of surprises!

Figure 2.2: Edmodo conversation with reading mentor.

Jada addresses this when she replies, "But I have a feeling that when Donavan finds out where he belongs he may start to be a good kid." Nardos also demonstrates understanding of Donovan's character. She replies, "Donavon is a good kid, he just doesn't know it yet!"

Rather than responding solely to their reading mentor, the students also interact with each other (see figure 2.3).

Claire said   *Sept. 25*

I noticed that the author uses some very dramatic language on p. 205:

"The heavy metal door was thrown open with such violence that it pounded against the cinder block wall. There, framed in the light from outside, was nothing less than an avenging angel."

What does the author mean by "avenging angel?" Do you all have any thoughts on this passage?

One more comment–In this chapter we also see how well Donovan has adjusted to his new school. He has really created a great community of friends. How does this affect him and his classmates when he has to leave? If I were a teacher, I would hope to have a class as close-knit as Donovan's!

Nardos said   *Sept. 29*

I think that "avenging angel" means a person who is like betraying or evil. Like maybe Donavan expected that some one bad was going to walk though those doors.

It appears almost as if everyone in the academy like Donavan, now even Abigail is warming up to him. Also I think that the robotics club really needs him now more than ever. That must have been terrifying for Chloe and all his friends there to see him get sent back to Hardcastle elementary!

Jada said   *Sept. 30*

I agree with Nardos because someone bad did walk through those doors, Shultz I also think the roboticts team needs him more than ever for the finals because I think they might fail without him.

Nardos said   *Sept. 30*

thanks Jada, and right now since they made it to the fainals they really need donavon

---

Nardos said   *Sept. 30*

Hey guys, who do you think helped Donavon pass the retest! I think its either chloe or abigial because sinse abigal hates him no one will suspect her and chloe like Donavon so much that she cut school to go find him! Who do you guys think did it?

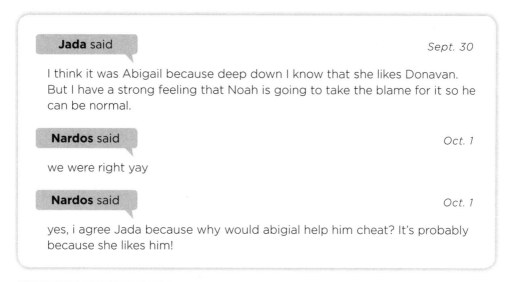

Jada said   *Sept. 30*

I think it was Abigail because deep down I know that she likes Donavan.
But I have a strong feeling that Noah is going to take the blame for it so he
can be normal.

Nardos said   *Oct. 1*

we were right yay

Nardos said   *Oct. 1*

yes, i agree Jada because why would abigial help him cheat? It's probably
because she likes him!

Figure 2.3: Reading mentor–facilitated Edmodo conversation with peers.

In the exchange featured in figure 2.3, students make predictions based on character motives and later either confirm or revise their thinking. Additionally, the students
demonstrate respect through polite comments such as "Thanks Jada" and "I agree
with. . . ." For instance, on October 1, Nardos agrees with Jada's prediction that Abigail
is the one who helps Donovan cheat.

Although Nardos' and Jada's Edmodo responses are frequent, thoughtful, and interactive in nature, other students' posts are limited. For example, recall Jamilet's conversations
with her reading mentor, Rebekah, at the opening of this chapter. From the beginning
of her online conversations with Rebekah, it is clear that Jamilet's posts are considerably
shorter than those of her peers. In the examples dated September 19 and September 29
(see figure 2.4, page 26), Jamilet's posts include one or two sentences, lack punctuation,
and typically respond to only one aspect of her reading mentor's posts.

In order to find an alternative means of communication to foster deeper engagement,
Rebekah incorporates a video response. In her video, Rebekah models her thinking aloud
to demonstrate the way she visualizes during reading. Not only does this increase Jamilet's
participation, but it helps improve her comprehension as well. In fact, after viewing
Rebekah's video, Jamilet reads, records her thinking on her own sticky notes, and then
creates her own video to show Rebekah how she applies the strategy to her independent
reading. This response is a great improvement from her earlier communications. Using
multimodal composition provides Rebekah and Jamilet with diverse ways to engage in
online communication.

Whether communicating with their peers or an outside reading mentor like preservice
teachers, digital tools such as Edmodo can offer students an online forum to interact with
text and peers to deepen their comprehension. Reading mentors play an important role
in helping students move beyond making generalizations such as "I like the book" by

> **Rebekah** said   *Sept. 18*
>
> I am really enjoying the book and I love reading about how
> determined Judy is to make a difference in the world. Sometimes
> her goals are a little unrealistic, but she helps readers realize that
> everyone is capable of helping the world become a better place.
> I was wondering what kinds of things are done at your school to
> help the environment. For example, does your school recycle or
> collect box tops? If you had to make a guess, who would you pre-
> dict is going to win the contest and take home the rollerblades?
> And how do you think the loser is going to react if they don't
> win? I was thinking how cool it would be if I got to design my own
> Band-Aid like Judy and Stink. If you have any free time maybe you
> could draw one too and we can attach pictures on Edmodo to
> show each other! I hope you are enjoying the book as much as me
> and I look forward to hearing back from you! Happy reading!
>
> **Jamilet** said   *Sept. 19*
>
> we do recycle box tops i think one of them are going to be mad if
> they do win the rollblades
>
> **Rebekah** said   *Sept. 26*
>
> Judy sure is taking extreme measures to save the world if she
> tried to live in a tree! Can you think of a time when you had to
> stand up for something you believed in?
>
> **Jamilet** said   *Sept. 29*
>
> yes i can stand up for something believed in

Figure 2.4: Rebekah's and Jamilet's Edmodo posts.

modeling and probing for more specific reactions and inferences with references to the text. At the conclusion of this experience, Nardos shares that she learned to ask herself questions and to figure out what the author is attempting to tell or show. She likes being able to ask her mentor about unknown words and talk about her reading by writing. She shares, "I feel like I have my own personal teacher!"

Understand Content Area Connections and Extended Applications

Teachers can easily integrate digital reader response into the content areas. For instance, students can create an Edmodo page for literary or historical figures. First, set up the account as if the character were the user and create posts from the character's point of view. Students can create multimedia presentations to depict story plots or historical events and show how the character or historical figure might respond or react accordingly. For instance, if a class is studying the American Revolution, students can create a profile from Paul Revere's perspective (see figure 2.5).

Figure 2.5: Paul Revere Edmodo profile.

As you can see, there is flexibility, using Edmodo in this way, that allows it to act as a central learning hub across multiple content areas.

Make Adaptations

Digital tools such as Edmodo enable the use of multimodal responses. This approach can meet learners' needs in any given classroom. For instance, students can respond to their reading through traditional written conversation, or they can record audio or video messages similar to what Jamilet and Rebekah did. ELs who are still developing proficiency with a second language may feel more comfortable and may be more successful by posting a visual response such as an illustration or image to Edmodo. Two options for uploading digital images can help students use Edmodo in this way. First, students may draw their illustrations on paper or create them in another medium and then upload a digital image of their illustration to Edmodo. Secondly, students can create a digital image using tools like Educreations or Scribble Press to illustrate and label their reader responses. As students develop their language skills, they can increasingly add text by labeling the illustrations, then writing simple sentences, and eventually articulating more complex ideas. Additionally, ELs can record their responses in their native language and begin to translate the components they know through labeling and writing.

Online Literature Discussions

"Students, it's time for independent reading. Pull out your books, and let's begin reading!" Mrs. Wiles directs her students and then grabs a self-selected book to model her own reading for her fourth graders. However, what she hears next is the daily chorus of queries and comments.

"I don't know what to read."

"Mrs. Wiles, Susie is using my crayons."

"What are we supposed to be doing right now?"

"I think I need to use the bathroom."

"I finished my book. Can I go to the library?

"Oooh, may I go to the library too?"

As an avid reader, Mrs. Wiles feels perplexed and frustrated with her students' lack of engagement during independent reading time. She wonders how she can increase student engagement and develop their motivation to read.

Mrs. Wiles is not alone. Although most teachers want students to be self-directed, engaged, and motivated to read, the reality is that many students become bored with the traditional reading process found in many schools of reading assigned texts and answering teacher-created questions. It is common to find struggling readers engaged in isolated skill and drill tasks rather than engaging with text in an authentic way (Allington, 2012; Dudley-Marling & Paugh, 2004). As a result, many of these students view reading as task-oriented rather than a meaning-making process and therefore lose interest and motivation (Stover, Sparrow, & Siefert, 2016). Engagement with a text, motivation to read, and student reading abilities are closely linked (Gambrell, 1996).

In this chapter, we'll explore how teachers can use classroom blogs to increase motivation to read. Blogging sites engage students in the blissful experience of reading a good book by fostering authentic, literature-based conversations and deepening comprehension.

Learn the Benefits of Digital Tools for Reading Comprehension and Motivation

Engaging students in the reading task carries special importance, as it "is strongly associated with reading achievement" (Guthrie & Wigfield, 2000, p. 404). *Reading engagement*, per Guthrie and Wigfield, can be defined as reading in a strategic and motivated manner, and therefore a significant component is motivation (Guthrie, Wigfield, & You, 2012). In fact, if students lack motivation to read, instruction in decoding, fluency, and comprehension is insufficient and students fail to become engaged and effective readers (Gambrell, 2011). One way that teachers can enhance students' motivation to read is to provide students with an authentic audience to discuss their reading (Allington & Gabriel, 2012; McCabe, 2009).

Ensuring that students have access to an authentic audience allows them to socially interact with others to think about and discuss the book they are reading (Allington & Gabriel, 2012; Gambrell, 2011; McCabe, 2009). While encouraging students to discuss what they are reading is a simple strategy and one that can have an enormous impact on students' comprehension, motivation, and language abilities, it is also one of the most underutilized approaches (Allington & Gabriel, 2012). An easy way to implement this strategy is to simply suggest that students turn and talk to one another before, during, and after reading a text (Gambrell, 2011). For example, before reading, students can turn and talk to a nearby classmate about predictions. While reading the text, students can discuss what they think might happen next or any questions that they are struggling with. After reading, students can discuss the ending of the text, ask questions, or make connections to other works that they have read.

With digital tools' increased availability, an authentic audience no longer needs to be limited to the students in the same classroom. Using technology brings an additional dimension to the practice of encouraging students to discuss text with an authentic audience. In fact, using digital tools allows any combination of students from elementary schools, middle schools, high schools, and universities, as well as members of the local or global community, to participate in an effective, authentic, literacy-based dialogue with one another (Mills & Levido, 2011).

Access Tools to Create Classroom Reading Blogs

A blog is one digital tool especially useful for encouraging 21st century communication between people near and far. Blogs provide users with a personal space to share content on the web. As Vicki L. Cohen and John E. Cowen (2011) define them, "Blogs are interactive web pages where individuals can post entries, articles, links and pictures, and ask others to join in conversations" (p. 51). The medium is well suited to classroom use for many purposes, such as posting book reviews, sharing class news, presenting student work, and responding to literature (Zawilinski, 2009). This digital space provides access to student work for a wider audience. For instance, students can communicate about their learning with their peers, families, and a more public audience beyond the classroom. Providing students with the opportunity to discuss their learning with authentic audiences can enhance motivation and engagement (Boling, Castek, Zawilinski, Barton, & Nierlich, 2008). Digital forums, such as blogs, can also improve students' communication skills while developing a sense of community (Larson, 2009).

There are a myriad of ways to implement blogs in the classroom setting. Many sites provide a free and safe platform for classroom blogging (table 3.1). What follows is an easy way to get started with blogging in the classroom.

Table 3.1: Digital Tools for Classroom Blogging

Tool and URL	QR Code	Description
Kidblog www.kidblog.org		Kidblog is a safe classroom blogging website where students can share their writing with an authentic audience.
Epals www.epals.com/#/connections		Epals is a safe and secure site that allows students to communicate and collaborate with classrooms around the world.
Edublogs https://edublogs.org		Edublogs is powered by WordPress and is a safe, free site that allows students and teachers to create blogs.
Quadblogging http://quadblogging.com		Quadblogging is free, and once the class is signed up, the site matches the class with three other classrooms from around the globe.

One classroom-friendly website, Kidblog, allows teachers to set up a classroom blog by assigning usernames and passwords to each student. In this way, only users with permission are able to log in to upload and read content. Students have the option to save blog posts they are composing. In the event that they run out of time before finishing a post, they can return to edit their blog posts at any time. Additionally, Kidblog requires the teacher to approve comments before they are posted. This allows the teacher to evaluate the appropriateness of comments, and to conference with and redirect students who post inappropriate content.

Transition to Digital Discussions About Reading Using Kidblog

We'll use Kidblog as our example, but the process of setting up a blog is much the same for the other websites in table 3.1 (page 31). Once a teacher selects a blogging website, he or she registers students and provides them (and their parents) with their login information and passwords. Now the class is ready to begin writing posts and comments. But how can teachers introduce students to blogging?

One way teachers can familiarize students with communicating in this digital space is to practice blogging together with them. For example, the teacher can have students craft an All About Me post as a way to introduce themselves. First, the teacher may want to begin by demonstrating his or her own All About Me blog post. This will provide a model for students while allowing them to get to know the teacher better. For instance, the teacher may include information about hobbies, family, favorite books, and perhaps a humorous or special memory. After modeling a blog post, the teacher demonstrates how to get started by showing students to use their username and password to log in, as well as how to post a comment. Next, students will craft their own All About Me posts over several class periods. It is helpful to provide ample time and support for students to post comments to one another's blogs. This helps students get to know their peers and build a sense of classroom community.

When designing their blog posts, students gain experience with different blog features. Many blogging sites allow students to choose backgrounds and font colors, as well as to insert photographs and clip art, which gives students a bit of ownership in the blog. Encourage them to explore and play with the various features of the blog to personalize their individual pages.

After students are familiar with the blogging website and its features, teachers can use blogs in a range of ways to facilitate students' authentic experiences with reading, writing, and communicating. For example, students can recommend favorite books or discuss a commonly read text (Moore, 2014; Zawilinski, 2009). Additionally, the class may decide to widen the audience by including others of similar, younger, or older ages within or beyond the school. One way to do so is by extending discussions to another classroom, using services such as those listed in table 3.1. This might include classrooms within the school, in other states, or even around the world.

Another way teachers can expand students' blogging experiences is to invite parents, community partners, or students from a university's education department to read and discuss the texts with students through the blog. Authentic conversations with authors and community leaders can become a reality with the use of a classroom blog.

Observe Digital Text Discussion Tools in Action

After learning about the importance of allowing students to discuss what they read, Mrs. Wiles, the technology leader in her school, decides to incorporate digital discussions in her classroom. Since she is fairly familiar with Kidblog, she selects the site to host her class blog. After adding each of her students as users, she constructs her own All About Me post to share with students. Then, Mrs. Wiles displays her All About Me post on the whiteboard (figure 3.1).

Mrs. Wiles said   *March 20*

My name is Mrs. Wiles. Welcome to my first blog post. I love teaching and have wanted to be a teacher since I was ten years old. My husband's name is Michael, and we have twin daughters, Isabelle and Stephanie. They just started kindergarten this year and they love it. I've lived in Arkansas for fifteen years. I moved to Fayetteville when I started at the University of Arkansas. Go Razorbacks!

My favorite thing to do is read. Some of my favorites include *Tales of a Fourth Grade Nothing* by Judy Blume and *Charlotte's Web* by E.B. White. I am reading *Bud, Not Buddy* by Christopher Paul Curtis right now. It's very funny. I have been laughing out loud so much that Michael asks me, "What is so funny?" What are some great books that you have read lately?

Figure 3.1: Mrs. Wiles' All About Me blog post.

After reading her post and having students share their initial thoughts, Mrs. Wiles shows her students how to use the comment feature on Kidblog. In this way, students can post comments and questions to one another. Mrs. Wiles also shows the students how to use the word-processing tools and then takes them to the computer lab so that they can begin their own All About Me posts. Students log in to their class Kidblog site and choose New Post to begin drafting their own All About Me posts. (See figure 3.2 for one student's example.)

Angel said   *March 22*

I am the oldest in my family. I have one younger brother. His name is Juan. Math is my favorite subject. I like working with fractions the most. I play soccer. We have our practices on Thursday and we play games on Saturday. We are the best team in all of Arkansas!

Figure 3.2: Angel's All About Me blog post.

Many students are fascinated with changing the font color, uploading pictures of their favorite novels, and reading their classmates' posts. Mrs. Wiles correctly thinks that this will be an appropriate time to remind students of the comment feature. "Remember, students, after you've finished your All About Me post, select Publish. Then, go back to the class blog page and read your friends' posts. You can even scroll to the bottom of your friend's post, write a comment, and select the Submit Comment button."

One of Angel's classmates, Sam, comments on her post: "Angel, I play soccer too! What position do you play? I am a forward. I like fractions too, but when we have to subtract, I get confused sometimes. Maybe we could study together?"

Mrs. Wiles encourages her students to read and respond to classmates' All About Me posts over the next two days. Then, when she feels that students are comfortable with the blog and the blogging process, Mrs. Wiles asks students to begin composing blog posts about their independent reading. Mrs. Wiles posts her thoughts about her independent reading book, *Out of My Mind* by Sharon Draper (2012), to provide students with an example (see figure 3.3).

> **Mrs. Wiles** said   *March 23*
>
> I am reading *Out of My Mind* by Sharon Draper. It's about a girl named Melody. She is so smart, but she can't talk. So nobody knows how smart she is. I made a text-to-self connection in that sometimes I have something really important to say, but I can't get it out. It just happens every once in a while though. I can't imagine never being able to communicate. I hope that Melody figures out a way to "speak her mind" soon. Are you reading a book where the main character has a problem? What is it?

Figure 3.3: Mrs. Wiles' blog post.

When modeling her own blog post for students, Mrs. Wiles explicitly highlights how her post provides a brief summary, connection, and discussion of the problem the character faces. She thinks aloud to show students how her post is conversational with the inclusion of questions for response. She provides students with a self-assessment rubric (figure 3.4, page 35) that is an easy-to-access reminder of the required blog components. She posts this rubric by the classroom computers and gives students copies to put in their readers' notebooks. Students seem to be excited about the prospect of writing about their books.

Once students are comfortable with this process, Mrs. Wiles provides them with an additional dimension to their thinking and learning. She contacts a local high school's Teacher Cadet program. Mrs. Wiles and the Teacher Cadet coordinator, Mr. Forman, discuss a possible partnership. When Mr. Forman talks about the partnership with his high school students who are interested in becoming teachers, they are excited about being able to connect digitally with elementary students.

> **I have included . . .**
>
> ☐ A short description of what I am reading
>
> ☐ A connection (text to text, text to world, or text to self)
>
> ☐ A prediction (what I think will happen next)
>
> ☐ A question for my readers to respond to

Figure 3.4: Self-assessment rubric for blogging.

Visit **go.SolutionTree.com/technology** *for a free reproducible version of this figure.*

Once Mrs. Wiles and Mr. Forman agree to have their classes blog together, they arrange the details of the partnership. First, the teachers pair each elementary student with a Teacher Cadet student. Then, the elementary students each choose an independent reading book. Mrs. Wiles approves the books and sends the selections to Mr. Forman. When he receives the list of elementary students and their book selections, Mr. Forman alerts his Teacher Cadet students to their elementary partners' book choices. Each Teacher Cadet finds a copy of his or her partner's text in the local library, purchases a copy from a local bookseller, or borrows the book from Mr. Forman's extensive collection.

Next, the elementary students write introductory posts to their Teacher Cadet buddies. In their introductory posts, the students follow a similar format to the All About Me posts and add what they were looking forward to discussing with their Teacher Cadet partners. The partners decide on a reading schedule and post every three days with updates on their thoughts, connections, and questions about the text.

As they respond to feedback from their Teacher Cadet buddies, students begin to demonstrate increased comprehension in their blog posts. For example, students are now posting thoughtful predictions, connections, and inferences. Not only does Mrs. Wiles notice increased comprehension with many of her students, she also observes that students seem more motivated to participate in the reading process. This project's format and the frequency of posting work well for Mrs. Wiles' and Mr. Forman's students, but they can be altered easily to suit the needs of any classroom.

In the joint blogging project with the Teacher Cadets and with the blogs her own classes establish, Mrs. Wiles finds blogging to be a useful tool for improving her students' reading skills. After implementing another class blog, Mrs. Wiles surveys her classroom and takes a deep breath. She sees three students at the classroom desktops, posting and commenting about books that they just finished. There are a few students reading at their desks, engrossed in their texts. She notices a student in the corner crafting a blog post on his iPad. Students are focused with a clear purpose. They are excited about sharing their book experiences with an authentic audience. Mrs. Wiles is no longer frustrated; she feels content with her students' engagement in the literacy process.

Understand Content Area Connections and Extended Applications

Online discussions are not limited to fictional texts. Students can read a section in a history book and discuss the information with one another on their blogs. For example, after reading a piece on the invasion of Normandy, students might discuss the merit of the decision to storm the beach. Questions to consider might include:

- Would I have done something different?
- Why or why wouldn't I have made the original decision?
- Would the outcome be changed?
- How would the outcome have changed if a different decision were made?

Students can also use classroom blogs as a space to discuss mathematics topics. The teacher can post a weekly word problem and encourage students to think about and post possible answers in the comment section. In science, students can post pictures of experiments as well as observations they make in the natural world. For example, if a class is studying weather's effects on the environment, the class might create a blog to share evidence of its findings. If a student sees an example of weathering on a walk to the park, he or she can take a photograph and upload it to his or her blog.

Make Adaptations

Blogging is versatile and can be adapted to suit all students' and classrooms' needs. Students can use the space as a class newsletter to inform their parents about what they are learning in school. Parents can ask questions or add to the discussion in the comment section. Teachers can post questions to the blog, where students can use the comment feature to weigh in on the debate. Instead of two or three students chiming in or dominating a class discussion, each student may craft a response and contribute to the discussion thoughtfully on a blog.

Blogs are also useful tools to address struggling students' needs. For example, ELs may feel uncomfortable when it comes to discussing a book or class event due to limited language proficiency. Allowing these students to blog in a digital space gives them additional time to gather and compose their thoughts. Then, the students can use the digital tools of spell-check, Google Translate, and so on to complete their posts. In this way, teachers may gain a more accurate perspective of ELs' knowledge and comprehension, as well as their abilities to apply what they have learned.

Additionally, blogs give struggling readers an opportunity to access authentic audiences that help to reinforce and support learning. For example, teachers may match struggling readers with members from the community or preservice teachers at neighboring universities. Providing each student with an online mentor makes targeted, individualized instruction more realistic and manageable.

PART II

Tools to Facilitate
Evaluation and Revision

Collaborative Evaluation of Online Sources

Juan, Trayvon, and Tim gather around a computer in the back of their fifth-grade classroom during reading workshop time. Assigned to work on a research project about the U.S. civil rights movement, they launch Internet Explorer and type "civil rights" into the search engine. It finds approximately 206 million results. Without much examination, the boys click on the first link, "Civil and political rights—Wikipedia, the free encyclopedia" ("Civil and Political Rights", 2015). After copying the first few sentences about civil rights in their notebooks, the students determine that the information is not specific to the civil rights movement in the 1950s and 1960s in the United States. So they decide to go back to their initial results page when Tim suggests they click on the link of images for civil rights. Upon noticing that most of the photos are in black and white, Juan remarks, "These look old school." Trayvon replies, "Yeah, look, that's Martin Luther King, Jr." Tim points out a photo with people holding a "We march for Selma" banner and chimes in, "Hey! Isn't there a movie called *Selma*?"

At this moment, the teacher (Mr. Carter) announces that the period is ending and students need to return to their seats. Without any information gathered, the boys decide to go back to the initial search results and click on the Wikipedia link. They print the results, write their names across the top, and submit it to the teacher's basket in the front of the classroom. Although the boys click on numerous photos and engage in some initial discussion, they have no written notes for their report on the civil rights movement by the time reading workshop ends.

Students like Juan, Trayvon, and Tim can easily feel overwhelmed when determining the importance of online content. We live in a time when information is plentiful, but determining what is relevant is increasingly difficult. Before the digital age, students traditionally relied on print sources, such as sets of encyclopedias, to provide them with information needed when conducting research. Often, readers consumed words in these texts without questioning the content or examining alternate sources. The digital world, however, has produced an overabundance of information at our fingertips. As a result of constantly developing technologies, new types of literacies emerge, requiring students to read and comprehend information in online spaces. Therefore, it is more important than ever to critically evaluate and synthesize information in online spaces.

In this chapter, we'll explore the use of online spaces to scaffold the research process for students and teach them how to critically evaluate online sources. We'll start by addressing the common use of online search engines to gather information from a vast array of sources and why it is paramount that students examine the relevancy and credibility of online content.

Learn the Benefits of Evaluating and Synthesizing Online Content

Schools commonly use the Internet to search for information (Eagleton, Guinee, & Langlais, 2003). According to Shenglan Zhang, Nell K. Duke, and Laura M. Jiménez (2011), "Even our youngest students have unprecedented access to information" (p. 158). With a click of a mouse or tap of a tablet, information is readily available. Yet, students must determine whether it is credible or not, as much of the information on the web is untrustworthy, outdated, and unfiltered. Unlike printed text, websites such as Wikipedia are often written by anonymous contributors whose credentials and expertise vary widely. Therefore, it is vital that students "learn how to critically evaluate websites to increase the likelihood that they are drawing on high-quality information" (Zhang et al., 2011, pp. 150–151).

In order for students to use the Internet to find information, they must be equipped with reading comprehension strategies (Henry, 2006). Julie Coiro (2003b) explains that for too long, many perceived the challenge of finding relevant information to be a technology-related issue rather than a comprehension issue. Rather than blaming technology, educators need to teach students skills and strategies to help them search for and evaluate online information (Coiro, 2003a). To move beyond simple information retrieval, it is necessary for students to learn how to comprehend information they find on the Internet (Coiro, 2003a; Leu, 2000). The International Literacy Association (2001) shares that many students lack the skills necessary to read and write in online spaces in the digital world. For instance, 70 percent of seventh graders in Coiro's (2014) study view online content as more important than credibility and rarely considered author or publication. In other words, many students did not consider the credibility of the source and consumed the material at face value without critique. The awareness and ability to evaluate online information is essential for learners of all ages (Zhang et al., 2011).

Without adequate reading skills to sort through the vast information on the web, students often begin their research by simply using the first online link available to them rather than reading the descriptions listed in the search results (Guinee, Eagleton, & Hall, 2003). It is easy to experience information overload with so many results from Internet queries (Henry, 2006). Additionally, since content is often extracted from multiple sources, each of which typically brings a unique perspective, it is necessary for students to learn how to synthesize online information to create a more complete picture than any one source can provide (Henry, 2006). As Laurie A. Henry (2006) posits, "The ability to search and locate information can be described as a gatekeeper skill in online reading" (p. 616). Readers, writers, and researchers must master these skills to successfully navigate the sheer number of sources available online.

Access Tools to Evaluate Online Content

In addition to sifting through the massive amount of information on the web, it is essential that students learn to evaluate its trustworthiness and credibility. The ability to find relevant and credible sources and synthesize this information to create new understanding is an essential lifelong skill needed for success in school and beyond (Zhang et al., 2011). Two digital tools, Blendspace and Symbaloo, are terrific aids for scaffolding the research process for students and helping them to evaluate the reliability of online content (table 4.1).

Table 4.1: Digital Tools for Scaffolding Research

Tool and URL	QR Code	Description
Blendspace website and app www.blendspace.com		Blendspace allows educators to create multimedia lessons by collecting numerous web resources in one online canvas they can easily share with a simple click or tap. It can be used to create learning modules to preteach content in a flipped classroom, to engage students in project-based learning, and to easily differentiate learning for students based on their instructional needs.
Symbaloo www.symbaloo.com		Symbaloo is a free digital bookmarking tool for visual resource management. It allows users to organize and share content online.
The Kentucky Virtual Library www.kyvl.org/kids/homebase .html		This website takes students step by step through the research process from planning to searching for information to note taking.

continued →

Gulf Coast State College Library's Video on Evaluating Websites https://youtu.be/aem3JahbXfk		This animated YouTube video shows students how to narrow search results and determine the credibility and reliability of online sources.
BrainPOP Online Sources www.brainpop.com/english /writing/onlinesources/preview .weml		BrainPOP is an online resource with educational videos and games. Although some videos are free, a subscription is necessary to access all resources. The video on the use of online sources is particularly useful in relation to the ideas discussed in this chapter.
"TILE SIG Feature: Resources for Teaching Critical Evaluation of Online Information" (Rhodes, 2013) http://literacyworldwide.org /blog/literacy-daily/2013/03 /22/tile-sig-feature-resources -for-teaching-critical-evaluation -of-online-information		This online teaching tip article provides educators with a description of how to teach students to critically evaluate online information. Links to resources are provided for further exploration.
Help Children Play and Stay Safe Online www.readwritethink.org/parent -afterschool-resources/tips -howtos/help-children-play -stay-30668.html		This website provides parents with tips and links to outside resources to keep kids safe online.
Skimming and Scanning: Using Riddles to Practice Fact Finding Online www.readwritethink.org /classroom-resources/lesson -plans/skimming-scanning -using-riddles-1079.html		This online lesson plan, which is focused more on process than critical evaluation, provides educators with suggestions for teaching students how to skim and scan websites to find relevant information.
"Identifying Reliable Sources and Citing Them" (Bunyi, 2010) www.scholastic.com/teachers /top-teaching/2010/11/reliable -sources-and-citations		This website provides educators with a series of lessons to develop students' abilities to identify and cite reliable online sources.

Blendspace is a website and app that allows educators to create multimedia lessons by collecting web resources in an online canvas they can easily share. Teachers can use it to create learning modules to preteach content in a flipped classroom, to engage students in project-based learning, and to easily differentiate learning for students based on their instructional needs.

This online tool is particularly useful when introducing students to research. Teachers can create a Blendspace as a scaffold for teaching students how to gather and evaluate information from online sources including text, audio, video, and infographics. The teacher predetermines the digital content and inserts it into the Blendspace. Depending on the space's intentional design, students click on the various links and complete the required tasks. For instance, the teacher may design a Blendspace to narrow online web searches for research projects. This is an effective way to provide students with limited choices when finding online content. Additionally, teachers can create a Blendspace with a combination of reliable and unreliable sources where students use a checklist to examine and evaluate each website. Eventually, students can create their own Blendspaces as a way to compile and present their learning about a given topic. Once students have conducted research, compiled notes, and synthesized the information, they can share their learning in an online canvas using Blendspace. Students can share any website on Blendspace's online canvas. This allows students to incorporate multimodal approaches to demonstrate their learning.

Symbaloo is another free digital bookmarking tool that is similar to Blendspace. This visual resource management tool allows users to organize and share content online. Once students are familiar with researching and evaluating websites, they can use Symbaloo to compile and share their own online sources. Symbaloo allows users to save more websites to the online canvas, making this a good option to create a collaborative place for students to share final projects.

Critical Evaluation of Online Sources

When introducing the concept of searching and evaluating online sources, it is helpful to have initial scaffolding in place. We begin by introducing students to the idea of online research using the Kentucky Virtual Library interactive website. This website takes students step by step through the research process, from planning to searching for information to note taking. Showing short video clips is another engaging approach to building students' background knowledge about any topic. The Gulf Coast State College Library's YouTube video on evaluating websites is a particularly student-friendly resource about critically assessing websites. (Visit **go.SolutionTree.com/technology** to access live links to the websites mentioned in this book.) The video shows students how common web searches can often produce too many irrelevant results and guides them in locating key indicators of a website's reliability.

You can easily insert websites such as the link from the Kentucky Virtual Library and the Gulf Coast State College Library YouTube video in a Blendspace canvas for a unit on how to research using the Internet. To get started, you will want to set up a free account with Blendspace. When you are ready to create your online canvas, click New Lesson.

This will take you to a blank canvas with six boxes for the online content. Click and drag your selected resources in each box. You can insert content including YouTube videos, Flickr images and videos, Educreations, webpages, images, and files from your computer, Dropbox, or Google Drive account. You may insert additional boxes for online content by clicking on the box titled Insert Row near the bottom of the screen. With all your online resources in one place, you are ready to give it a title and share the content with others.

Observe Blendspace and Web Searches in Action

An online search for information is a complex process and students benefit from a structured approach using Internet workshops (Leu, 2000). Using an Internet workshop within his literacy block, Mr. Carter designs a series of lessons to teach his fifth graders about searching for and evaluating information on the Internet. The series of lessons addresses the National Governors Association Center for Best Practices and the Council of Chief State School Officers (NGA & CCSSO, 2010) Common Core State Standards for English language arts anchor standard eight for writing: Research to build and present knowledge—"Gather relevant information from multiple print and digital sources, assess the credibility and accuracy of each source, and integrate the information while avoiding plagiarism" (CCRA.W.8). He begins by asking his students to raise their hands to indicate if they use the Internet. All hands immediately shoot up. Next, he asks students to raise their hands if they use the Internet to read. Most students raise their hands. He then prompts students to consider how online reading differs from print reading. Responses from students include that online reading is "more interesting," "gives faster access," "has more real-world topics," and "there's lots more information online."

Mr. Carter displays the Blendspace he created for this lesson. The first link on the Blendspace canvas includes a shared Google Docs document where the students find a two-column chart with the headers Reliable Resources and Unreliable Resources. Mr. Carter displays the chart and then asks his class, "What do you know about the terms *reliable* and *unreliable*?"

"My friend Josh is reliable because I can count on him," Juan replies.

"The bus is reliable because it picks me up at the same time every day," Sheron adds.

Mr. Carter responds, "Yes, good examples, Juan and Sheron. The information we find on the Internet may or may not be reliable. In other words, we need to determine if we can count on it to be accurate and trustworthy."

Mr. Carter clicks on the Blendspace to go to the second online resource. He shows stu-

dents a BrainPOP video to introduce reliable and unreliable sources (see table 4.1, page 42). This helps activate students' background knowledge and creates a shared experience for the lesson. The students take notes using the two-column chart in Google Docs (see table 4.2, page 45). Then, they engage in a discussion about their new understanding.

Table 4.2: Mr. Carter's Class-Created Chart About Reliable and Unreliable Sources

Reliable Resources	Unreliable Resources
Sources that we can trust and that give accurate information	Sources that may not be trustworthy and may give incorrect information
<ul><li>Is up to date (depends on the topic)</li><li>Has a credible author or publisher</li><li>Gives accurate information: cross-check facts</li><li>Looks professional</li><li>May have a URL ending with .edu, .org, or .gov</li></ul>	<ul><li>Is usually biased: author gives opinion too strongly and tries to convince readers</li><li>Has a URL ending with .com</li><li>Has advertisements</li><li>Has other characteristics that include the exact opposite of reliable resources (for example, gives inaccurate information)</li></ul>

After discussing the shared notes about credible sources, Mr. Carter uses a scaffolded approach with the 5Ws of website evaluation to model a step-by-step process for critically evaluating webpages (see figure 4.1). He wants to teach students to become detectives as they search for information online. Although a website may appear to look professional and authentic, the content may not always be accurate. Before releasing students to begin online research, Mr. Carter gives explicit instruction on selecting a focused topic for online searches and provides scaffolding using the 5Ws to teach his students fundamental skills to search and evaluate online sources. The 5Ws are an easy way to remember questions to consider when critically evaluating online sources. In addition to using the 5Ws, Mr. Carter teaches his students to cross-reference content for accuracy and consistency through examination of at least three websites.

> Use the 5Ws to evaluate a website's credibility before using the website information for schoolwork or personal use.
>
> 1. Who wrote the piece? What are the author's credentials?
> 2. What is the purpose of this site? What information is included in this site?
> 3. When was the site created? When was it last updated?
> 4. Where is the information from?
> 5. Why was this information written? Why is this page more useful than other websites?

Figure 4.1: The 5Ws for website evaluation.

Next, Mr. Carter gathers his students together and displays an Internet search engine on the Smart Board. As Mr. Carter types his topic into the search engine, he explains, "My purpose for conducting this online search is to find information on endangered animals." As expected, when he types "endangered animals" into the search engine, infinite results appear. "Wow, there are just too many results here. I'm mostly interested in the endangered animals of the United States. So, I'm going to add those words to narrow my results." Mr. Carter types "endangered animals in the United States." He scrolls through the list of results on the first page and models aloud his thinking about which websites to select.

"As I look at the actual websites and the content listed in the description, I think Earth's Endangered Creatures looks like a good website to begin my research. I like how this website offers a search feature for endangered animals based on geographic region."

Mr. Carter goes to the website and scrolls through the long list of animals. He finally reaches the bottom of the website where the copyright and several additional links appear. He wants to know where the information comes from to determine if the information is trustworthy.

"The first thing I observed is that the website is current based on the date at the bottom of the page. I also noticed a link titled About EEC. I will click there to learn more about who created this website. I appreciate the disclaimer that states that there are many organizations that create lists and how EEC is willing to update its website with user feedback."

After sufficient modeling and practice as a class, Mr. Carter directs his students to evaluate the website Pacific Northwest Tree Octopus (http://zapatopi.net/treeoctopus). He chooses this website specifically because it was created as a hoax solely for this type of exercise; the Pacific Northwest tree octopus does not exist. Mr. Carter explains that he wants the students to practice using the skills for evaluating websites while working in pairs. Collaboratively, students employ the 5Ws framework as they examine the selected website. When conducting research, Mr. Carter's students apply the strategies to evaluate other online sources and gather credible and relevant information.

Understand Content Area Connections and Extended Applications

Third-grade teacher Ms. Becker integrates social studies content within her literacy block to extend students' understanding. Throughout a unit on the Underground Railroad, students are fully immersed in learning as they read a range of print and online texts during independent reading, guided reading, and computer time. While some students meet with Ms. Becker for guided reading instruction, student pairs gather to read books related to the Underground Railroad. Meanwhile, other students rotate through the computer station where they work in small groups to explore additional information online about the Underground Railroad.

To help her students access relevant sites, Ms. Becker creates a Blendspace to scaffold her students' research process when studying the Underground Railroad (see figure 4.2). Students log into the Blendspace to explore the websites Ms. Becker selected or play the game *Journey to Freedom*.

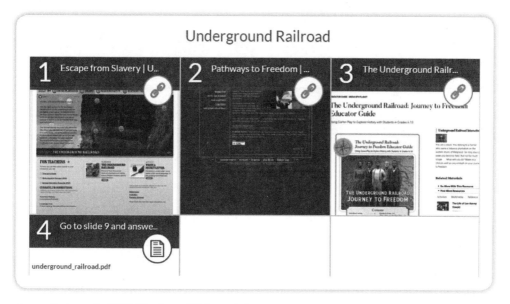

Source: Becker, n.d., 2016; Blendspace. With permission.

Figure 4.2: Underground Railroad Blendspace canvas.

Students read a variety of print and digital informational texts with a particular research focus in mind. Specifically, Ms. Becker's students examined the Underground Railroad from different perspectives such as the slaves', plantation owners', and slave hunters'. Students carefully evaluate online content and conduct research and then work together to create perspective books about the Underground Railroad. For instance, when read one way, the reader learns about the Underground Railroad from the slave's perspective. When flipped over, the information is conveyed from the plantation owner's point of view. This standards-based approach allows students to deepen their knowledge of the subject they are studying. CCSS anchor standard seven for writing suggests the need for students to conduct research to demonstrate understanding of the subject being studied (NGA & CCSSO, 2010). Prior to engaging in this research, students in Ms. Becker's class had limited understanding of the Underground Railroad. In fact, several students had misconceptions, thinking that it was literally an underground railroad, like a subway. Through reading a variety of online sources, students deepened content knowledge in social studies.

Make Adaptations

Teaching students to understand and distinguish between reliable and unreliable online resources is a vital, lifelong skill for research both in and out of the classroom setting, formally and informally.

A faster, more informal approach to the 5Ws for website evaluation can be framed around the idea of *keeping it REAL*. REAL is an acronym that can help students recall vital steps for examining online content (figure 4.3).

Read the URL.

Examine the content.

Ask about the author.

Look at the links.

Figure 4.3: Keeping it REAL.

Mr. Carter explains to his students that he uses this process when he is looking for information on his own. He gave students the example last week, when he heard a bunch of cicadas in his yard. He was interested in learning about these creatures, so he turned to the Internet for answers. After searching for information using the key word *cicada*, he read (R) the URL. He reminds his students that many reliable websites end in .com, .edu, and .gov. Yet, this is not always the case, and consequently it is essential that students critically evaluate the content. Next, Mr. Carter demonstrates how he examines (E) the web content. Afterward, he asks (A) about the author's credentials. Finally, he looks (L) at links and checks several places to examine the copyright, how recently it was published, and determines if the information is trustworthy. Keeping it REAL is an easy-to-remember approach students can use when searching for online content in the real world.

Online Book Reviews

Ms. Derrick hears audible sighs, along with remarks such as "Do we have to?" and "I don't like writing" when she announces to her third-grade class that it's time for writing. Many of these third graders aren't interested or motivated when it comes to traditional forms of writing, and some are reluctant to write altogether. However, when Ms. Derrick explains that they will be writing and sharing book reviews on the Internet, students' responses are suddenly enthusiastic and full of life. Students energetically exclaim, "How cool!" and "I can't wait to get started!" They quickly became more engaged in the learning experience because they know the end product isn't just a piece of writing to be filed away. Instead, they know others, including their family members, will be able to view and hear their work.

Using websites such as audioBoom to record reading of their written book reviews, as well as Twitter and QR codes to provide instant access to their audioBoom links, increases students' confidence.

Like Ms. Derrick's students, many learners find their desire to produce quality work grows when they realize an authentic audience will listen. Digital tools allow students to focus more on the content of their writing rather than just surface features or conventions that often limit the writing quality. In this chapter, we'll explore how to make the leap from traditional forms of book reviews to online book reviews using digital audio recording websites and social media platforms.

Learn the Benefits of Using Digital Tools for Book Reviews

The traditional response to reading a book can take such forms as written book reports, dioramas, and oral class presentations. Sharing understandings and ideas about books is certainly not novel. However, the audience for these reports rarely extends beyond the teacher, and students view book reports as simply another task to complete. Therefore, students often demonstrate a lack of interest in book report writing (Carlsen & Sherrill, 1988; Krieger, 1991/1992, as cited in Reinking & Watkins, 2000).

With the advent of the Internet, technology use has expanded the forum and audience for students to share about books. Research suggests that reading and writing in digital spaces provides students with opportunities for more meaningful communication (Beach & Lundell, 1998; Bruce & Rubin, 1993; Garner & Gillingham, 1996, 1998; Myers, Hammett & McKillop, 1998; Turner & Dipinto [1992] as cited in Reinking & Watkins, 2000). Digital spaces allow students to use a range of modalities to share information about books, including text, images, audio and video clips, and hyperlinks to authors' websites or online marketplaces where readers can purchase their own copy of the book. Multimedia book reviews offer an alternative to the often criticized traditional book report. David Reinking and Janet Watkins (2000) note the impact technology has on the audience and interest level: "Unlike book reports that are often written only for the teacher, multimedia book reviews as digital documents naturally lend themselves to being shared by a larger audience that might include other students, parents, or even the World Wide Web" (p. 389).

Twenty-first century tools have changed book reviews from being one-dimensional to more collaborative and accessible to a wider audience. No longer do book reviews need to be limited to only literary authorities. According to Barbara Hoffert (2010), editor of *Library Journal*'s Prepub Alert, "Reviewing is no longer centralized, with a few big voices leading the way, but fractured among numerous multifarious voices found mostly on the web" (p. 23). Students experience the power of their voices as they share about books with a wider audience. Reinking and Watkins's (2000) study reveals several benefits when students created and shared multimedia book reviews. First, students improved their social interactions and attitudes toward reading, leading to increased time spent reading independently. Additionally, students gained confidence and self-esteem, which led to improved engagement in literacy-related activities. Lastly, results reveal that the multimedia book review activities stimulated creativity among the high-achieving readers (Reinking & Watkins, 2000). Sharing in digital spaces fosters a wider sense of audience. Receiving responses from an authentic audience, including likes, shares, and comments, helps students develop a sense of purpose for their work. According to Seung Won Park (2013), "The immediate feedback can empower students to perceive active interactions and feel respected, which promotes their engagement" (p. 51).

Access Tools That Help Make Book Reviews Engaging

Students can easily use several common digital tools to support and share online book reviews. Table 5.1 (page 51) offers a brief overview of many tools suitable for classroom use, including audioBoom podcasts, QR codes, and Twitter.

Table 5.1: Digital Tools for Online Book Reviews

Tool and URL	QR Code	Description
audioBoom www.audioboom.com		An easy-to-use online platform, audio-Boom can be used in educational settings to record and share podcasts with peers, parents, and people from around the world.
Kaywa QR Code https://qrcode.kaywa.com/		Kaywa allows users to freely create an unlimited number of static QR codes. A paid version allows users to create dynamic, trackable QR codes. Users simply paste a URL address, and the website automatically generates the QR code that can be downloaded or copied and pasted into another document or online source.
QR Reader https://itunes.apple.com /us/app/qr-reader-for -iphone/id368494609 ?mt=8		This is a free QR reader app for iPhones. Users can simply scan QR codes, barcodes, and documents to have instant access to information.
QR Stuff www.qrstuff.com		This free website allows users to easily create QR codes and download them for immediate use.
QR Code Generator www.the-qrcode-generator .com		Users create a QR code by selecting a function for the code (such as URL, Facebook link, or PDF), enter the content, and then download or print the instantly created QR code.
Twitter https://twitter.com		Twitter is an online social media network that allows users to create a profile and connect with a wider audience. Once users create their profiles, they can compose and share short 140-character messages, or *tweets*, with their followers. The use of the hashtag symbol (#) categorizes tweets to make it easier for users to find specific topics. Many teachers are now creating class profiles on Twitter for educational purposes.

An easy-to-use online platform, audioBoom can be used in educational settings to record and share podcasts with peers, parents, and people from around the world. The free version of audioBoom allows users to post an unlimited number of audio recordings, or *boos*, up to ten minutes in length. For a fee, users can post their recordings to iTunes. Both versions include an option to follow, comment, or send direct voice messages to other users. Students can share their boos easily with a wide audience by embedding the link in a blog, posting the link on Twitter or Facebook, or creating a QR code directly within the audioBoom website.

In this chapter, we discuss the use of QR codes to create links to students' audioBoom podcasts of book reviews.

Additionally, this chapter discusses the use of Twitter as a way to connect with, follow, and share information with other students, educators, and people from around the world. (Refer to the description in table 5.1, page 51.) In the following example, students are asked to write a 140-character review, including hashtags such as #readergrams or #5stars, a photo of the book cover, or a link to their audioBoom podcast review. When tweeting about books, students can include the published authors in their conversations, which can invigorate students' book discussions and deepen their examination of the authors' craft (Messner, 2009). In these ways, Twitter provides students with a digital space to connect with other readers and authors to share and discuss books.

Transition to Digital Book Reviews

The creation of digital book reviews has many benefits. First, when students write a review of a text, they begin by summarizing and sharing their opinion. Not only does this meet multiple standards for reading and writing, but when students record audio of their written reviews, they practice speaking skills. Students typically desire to listen to the recordings immediately and then naturally self-evaluate their written expression and oral fluency. This often leads to an organic revision process before publishing for a live audience on the web.

As with any other type of writing, it is helpful to start by sharing examples of mentor texts with students. Begin by showing students samples of book reviews on websites such as Amazon or Goodreads. Read the reviews to students and think aloud about what you notice about the structure and content of the review. Elicit participation from students and record collective observations on an anchor chart for students to reference at a later time when writing their own reviews. Next, model writing your own review using these elements studied in the mentor text example. During a follow-up lesson, students can participate in a shared writing experience to create a review for a common read-aloud. Explain that reviews can be an effective way to recommend books to their peers. Once students have ample opportunities with practicing writing reviews, show them how to publish their reviews online to reach a wider audience.

Just as with any type of technology, it is important to introduce the digital tool and demonstrate procedures for use. Begin by showing students how to log in and create an audio file. This can be done on the computer or with the free app on an iPad. Click on the red record icon to upload or record a file. To record a file, click on the word Record and the red button. When finished, click pause and playback to review. Recordings can be discarded or saved accordingly. Add a title and image and then publish the completed file. After the file is saved, it can be shared on a number of platforms, including audioBoom, Facebook, Twitter, and Google. (Visit **go.SolutionTree.com/technology** to access live links to all websites mentioned in this book.)

Observe Online Book Reviews in Action

Third-grade teacher Ms. Derrick wants to give her students authentic and engaging opportunities for writing while broadening their reading repertoires. Therefore, she introduces students to writing online book reviews. They begin by studying several online examples, including book reviews written by kids at Spaghetti Book Club: Book Reviews by Kids for Kids (www.spaghettibookclub.org), and previewing several book trailers. By examining different types of online reviews, the students are better equipped to determine what information is important to include and how they want to write their own book reviews. They discuss and compare qualities of good reviews. In fact, the third graders are rather disappointed when a review for *The Boxcar Children* (Warner, 1989), a book they are reading, reveals the end of the story. As a result, the students come to consensus that they will not include book endings in their own reviews to avoid spoiling the book for potential readers.

Additionally, when previewing the book trailers, students critique the narrator's lack of fluency and conclude that in order to appeal to potential readers, they need to be expressive. After drafting their written book reviews, the students practice reading their reviews with a partner. They coach each other and offer tips such as when and how to slow down, pay attention to end punctuation to indicate appropriate intonation, and change their tone of voice to convey the intended meaning to their audience.

In her book review for Daisy Meadows's (2011) *Nia the Night Owl Fairy*, Lily states, "The owl led Kristy and Rachel to their fairy village, where their fairy friends were. Then, they saw something horrible! What did Kristy and Rachel see at the fairy village?" (Derrick3RD, n.d.). After listening to Lily read her review multiple times, her partner suggests that Lily emphasize her pronunciation of the word *horrible* and then pause for effect. She also compliments Lily on the way that she uses intonation when asking the question at the end. After working together, Lily's partner exclaims, "Ms. Derrick, you *have* to hear Lily read this! It sounds *so* good!" This level of enthusiasm is rare. In fact, Lily's partner is so excited that she quickly becomes invested in Lily's project as well as her own.

After peer feedback and revision, the third graders are ready to share their book reviews and convince others to read their books. To reach a wider audience, they record their reviews, using audioBoom, on iPad minis and then listen to their recordings together. After listening to their recordings, most students want to rerecord a second, third, fourth, or even fifth time to make it better. Once the book reviews are published on audioBoom, the students create QR codes to share their book reviews with their peers. Ms. Derrick updates the traditional bulletin board in the classroom that displays book reviews written on sticky notes to include QR codes that students can scan with the iPads to link to the student-created audioBoom book reviews. This interactive and multimodal display allows students to share their opinions of beloved books with a wider audience. In fact, Ms. Derrick invites parents and community members to scan the QR codes and hear the students' reviews when they attend PTA and school board events.

In an effort to share students' book reviews with a broader audience beyond PTA meetings and school functions, Ms. Derrick encourages students to tweet their book reviews using the hashtag #readergrams. She begins by asking students to write their tweets using paper and pencil. Then they take their picture holding their favorite books and share their book reviews on Twitter using #readergrams. Students also tweet links to their audioBoom podcast book reviews. The students are so excited to receive notifications when other classes follow them and like and comment on their tweets.

Recording book reviews on audioBoom and sharing the reviews using QR codes and Twitter offers numerous benefits, including improved motivation, enhanced fluency, and increased risk taking as writers. This experience boosts students' confidence and overall fluency as both readers and writers. Some of the struggling readers in Ms. Derrick's class make great strides in their reading abilities as a result of the purposeful repeated reading experiences. Her students take ownership of the partner reading and feedback exercises. As they practice reading aloud their book reviews to their peers, they continually make revisions, and the quality of their writing improves. This is a shift from the typical rush just to get something written and be done with it. The multiple readings encourage students to think about their work and examine whether they are conveying meaning effectively. For instance, students hesitate to use words they do not know how to spell in their writing. However, knowing that they would be sharing their work using multimodalities such as audio, students feel at ease, are more confident in their word choice, and take greater risks with vocabulary usage. See "7 Ways to Use #readergrams With Students" on Teachivity (http://goo.gl/OpphLQ) for more information on #readergrams.

Understand Content Area Connections and Extended Applications

The digital tools we discuss in this chapter can be incorporated into the classroom in numerous ways. For instance, students can use Twitter to share an exit slip at the end of a science or social studies lesson to demonstrate their understanding of content knowledge. They can post pictures on Twitter to display various ways they worked out a mathematics problem and elicit conversation with others to discuss problem solving. By sharing learning using social media, students reach a larger audience and increase their chance of getting a response. Research shows the value of social interaction as a way to enhance and deepen understanding (Vygotsky, 1978). Furthermore, the teacher can monitor students' digital exit slips to determine any misconceptions and needs for reteaching or enrichment in all subject areas.

Teachers can post QR codes throughout the classroom to engage students in a *gallery crawl* activity to get them up and moving. When participating in a gallery crawl, the teacher creates stations around the room where the students rotate to experience each station with their peers during a given period of time. In this case, students rotate through stations containing different QR codes linked to websites and activities related to the instructional objectives and activities. Each QR code can take them to a website with information about a given topic. For instance, when studying communities, second graders scanned QR codes to read about and take notes on a variety of local municipalities and organizations. Teachers can use QR codes to provide students with access to a range of differentiated mathematics problems or leveled text. Students might also scan a QR code displayed on a Smart Board for morning work activities. We encourage you to talk with your colleagues and students and consider other ways to incorporate these digital tools to foster sharing of student work and understanding in your own classrooms. You could even tweet about it to share with other educators! Twitter is a great way for teachers to gain access to insight and resources other professionals share (Ferriter, 2010).

Make Adaptations

The digital tools we discuss in this chapter help engage students in learning. Instead of painstakingly hand-writing or word-processing every assignment, struggling writers can use audioBoom to record their voices to contribute to the class conversations. Students can then generate a QR code or post their link to Twitter. With its low character limit and ability to represent thoughts with images, Twitter may also help to alleviate some of the stress that struggling writers face. Using QR codes around the classroom or even outside fosters movement and helps increase student engagement.

Additionally, in order to represent their understanding of a specific concept, ELs can create images to convey meaning. These images might take the form of diagrams in science or steps for mathematical problem solving. Using the camera on a tablet, students can take a photo of these drawings to post to Twitter. They can also label their images through written response on Twitter.

6

Digital Revision

"Emile, why are you already back in your seat?" Ms. Jarriel questions.

"I'm finished reading Nancy's story," Emile replies. He looks at Ms. Jarriel with surprised eyes. Why is she questioning him? As Nancy's writing buddy, Emile read her story. He thought it was good and told her so. He did what he is supposed to and even returned to his seat to work on other projects.

Ms. Jarriel approaches Nancy, who is leaving the writing corner on the move back to her seat. "Nancy, may I see your first draft?"

As Nancy hands her teacher the first draft of her story, she smiles. She is finished and looks forward to handing it in and receiving praise from her teacher.

"All right, Emile. You and Nancy come sit with me for a moment. Let's talk about your revision process," Ms. Jarriel says.

The students join Ms. Jarriel at the writing table. Ms. Jarriel looks at Emile and asks, "Why didn't you write any feedback on sticky notes for Nancy? I wonder if you have some comments or even some suggestions for how she could make this piece of writing even better?"

Emile shrugs. "I didn't need to . . . It's good . . . I like it."

Ms. Jarriel sighs. As a veteran teacher, she has heard this phrase one too many times. She spends countless days providing her students with revision strategies in her writing minilessons. Yet, many times, their first response is to say "It's good" or "It's perfect" or even "I like it."

"How do we move beyond 'I like it'?" she wonders.

To the disappointment of writing teachers everywhere, many students avoid revising their work. Like Ms. Jarriel, most teachers understand the struggle of encouraging students to engage in the practice of revision. It is not unusual for students to avoid authentic revision at all costs (Angelillo, 2005; Fletcher, 2013), often because they are unfamiliar with how to revise their work (Heard, 2002). While it may be disheartening the first time a student takes a handwritten rough draft, replaces a couple words with synonyms, and copies it over in ink to hand in as a final copy, there is hope. In fact, there are ways in which teachers can demonstrate the importance of revision as they support students in their efforts to revise.

In this chapter, we explore how using Google Docs to provide students with authentic feedback can enhance the revision process and overall writing quality.

Learn the Benefits of Using Digital Tools to Reframe Revision

To help students embrace revision, educators can begin by reframing the purpose of revision in students' minds. According to Murray (1999b), "Beginning writers sometimes think revision is punishment" while "experienced writers see revision as opportunity" (p. 202). Students must understand that revision is not a way to fix a bad piece of writing but a way to make a good piece of writing even better (Fletcher, 2013). Specifically, students need to know that "rewriting is not a failure but an essential part of the process of writing; each draft leads us to our meaning and allows us to tune our voices to that meaning" (Murray, 1999a, p. 56).

While often used synonymously, revision and editing are different processes. *Revision* is a continuous process that encompasses thinking about the audience, deciding if an idea is sufficiently fleshed out, and considering word choice (Fountas & Pinnell, 2001). *Editing* is more about polishing the work (Angelillo, 2005) and often involves the line-by-line, word-by-word mechanics of correcting spelling, adding punctuation, and conforming to published standards. Google Docs is a useful tool to foster revision and editing through synchronous and asynchronous communication and collaboration with other writers. Technology can reframe the revision process, resulting in greater student engagement. No longer will students lament about copying over their work by hand, a regular occurrence even in modern classrooms. Rather, they can log into tools such as Google Docs to share and obtain feedback and make meaningful and more efficient digital revisions. Digital revision allows students to make changes by adding, removing, and rearranging text without having to recopy the first draft, a laborious, unauthentic process that leaves hands tired and students frustrated. Students can provide and receive asynchronous peer feedback within the margins of the school day and beyond, not just during writing workshop.

Whether during morning work, when classwork is complete, or outside of school hours, students can use technology to access their work in progress or read their peers' work and leave comments. These comments can be resolved through revision or can become part of a dialogic conversation with the author. For instance, a peer may leave a comment asking for clarification or greater details in a particular section of the text. Students can also communicate synchronously through chat features within the live document.

Access Tools to Engage Students in Synchronous and Asynchronous Revision

Providing and receiving authentic feedback is integral to a writing community as well as individual writers. In years past, students typically gave feedback in one of two ways. First, students gave one another oral feedback. This became problematic when students forgot what was suggested. Second, students provided comments to peers in a handwritten form and it could be a struggle to interpret classmates' handwriting. Additionally, providing each student with feedback in an oral or handwritten form can be a time-consuming process. New web tools make this communication process easier (see table 6.1).

Table 6.1: Digital Tools for Providing Feedback

Tool and URL	QR Code	Description
Microsoft Word Online https://office.live.com/start/Word.aspx		An online version of the popular program Microsoft Word, this site allows users to collaborate in real time to write, revise, and share documents.
Google Docs www.google.com/docs/about		This free tool enables users to create and edit documents collaboratively in a shared online space. Users can invite others to access the shared document.

Now, from the convenience of any computer or tablet with an Internet connection, writers can asynchronously glean feedback through comments in the margins of their shared documents. This makes communication between writers and readers from both near and far much easier. As opposed to traditional static word-processing programs like Microsoft Word that require writers to send a document back and forth, web-based tools like Microsoft Word Online and Google Docs allow users to simultaneously work in the shared space. The author can simply share access to any documents with a broader audience, including a teacher and peers. The feedback and revision process can begin easily with a click of a mouse or tap of a screen at any time from anywhere, making it more convenient for writers to communicate and collaborate with others. All writing and comments are automatically saved, and the writing's revision history can be viewed at any time by clicking on a link under the File tab. Additionally, Google Docs offers a chat feature for conversations in real time. The user simply clicks the small square with the text box, located next to the comment button, in the upper-right corner to get started.

Let's take a closer look at how to begin using Google Docs in the classroom.

Transition to Revision Using Google Docs

Google Docs can be used in a myriad of ways in the classroom. We suggest displaying a previously created document on the Smart Board to demonstrate the comment feature to students. Once the document is displayed for the students to see, follow these steps.

1. Read the work aloud and begin a discussion with students about the text. You may want to model how you answer questions such as What do you like? Where are you confused? How could the piece be revised?
2. Highlight a piece of text that was identified as needing revision. This can be as small as a character or as large as an entire paragraph.
3. Click on Insert, then Comment (or click the Comment symbol that appears in the margin next to the highlighted text)
4. Once the box opens up, select Comment from the menu. A small box will appear next to the highlighted text.
5. Demonstrate how to enter appropriate feedback.
6. Click the Comment button to save your feedback.

When the author reads through the comments, she has the option to click on the comment box and reply by typing her thoughts into the text box. Or, if she agrees with the feedback and it is fairly easy to implement, she can choose Resolve, and the comment can no longer be seen on the page. However, all comments are stored. Click the Comment button at the top right of the screen to see a running list of them.

When you begin teaching your students to revise using Google Docs, there are a few helpful tips to consider. Depending on your students' ages and typing abilities, you may want to begin with a small piece of text or even allow students to revise a piece of familiar text. As soon as students have a section of text typed into the Google Docs file, they can begin leaving feedback for one another. Ms. Jarriel supplies her students with sentence starters to provide some scaffolding. For example, her students can respond, "I like how you . . ." and "To make it even better. . . ." Once students are in the habit of providing feedback, the sentence starters can be phased out. Additionally, it is important to inform your students that the text they are placing in the Google Docs file will be revised with peers.

Let's check in with Ms. Jarriel's students to see how they use Google Docs to collaborate with their peers, receive feedback, and improve their writing.

Observe Google Docs in Action

During guided reading, Ms. Jarriel works with a group of three boys who have similar reading strengths and areas of needed growth. All three students decode well but struggle with fluency and reading motivation. Ms. Jarriel incorporates a reader's theater activity to target reading, comprehension, writing, spelling, and fluency. In this case, students revise a familiar story by reformulating it into a reader's theater script along with their own text revisions.

To begin the lesson, Ms. Jarriel reads the book *Tough Boris* by Mem Fox (1994) aloud. Due to the text's short and repetitive nature, students easily revise the story by adding in dialogue. Ms. Jarriel discusses how the original story does not have any speaking parts or dialogue. She identifies the characters for the script and provides an example of how to create dialogue for the main character, Tough Boris. She models an appropriate line for Tough Boris using a pirate's voice, "Aaarrghhh mateys, I am the largest pirate in the land!" Each student is given a typed copy of *Tough Boris* with different sections highlighted. This is the section of the script each student will revise using Google Docs to simultaneously add dialogue to his section of the reader's theater script.

Ms. Jarriel explains the purpose and procedure of giving effective peer feedback and shows a chart of the two types of feedback (positive compliments and helpful suggestions) written as the sentence starters "I like how you . . ." and "To make it even better . . ." She discusses ideas for the types of suggestions to offer as well as encourages the students to be as specific as possible. Ms. Jarriel points students' attention to the board, where she writes a sample line of the script in order to model how to revise it to add detail and pirate language. She discusses the *show, not tell* strategy in terms of writing dialogue that reveals Tough Boris's character traits rather than simply restating the adjectives.

As Ms. Jarriel starts to model, she asks the students how a pirate could *show* he is tough, not just say "I'm so tough." She uses a sentence starter like "I'm so tough that I . . ." Tyler and Aiden chime in with examples of toughness, such as fighting other pirates and beating a T-Rex. Ms. Jarriel incorporates their ideas into the revised modeled on the board. Next, she introduces a second sentence starter, "One time I . . .," to show students how they can include examples in their dialogue of things that Tough Boris may have done in the past. Although you won't be able to see the colors in figure 6.1 (page 62), these revisions are written in blue below the original dialogue to illustrate how much more detailed and specific the revised line can be. Ms. Jarriel uses a green marker to model how to add pirate language ("Aaargh") to the script. Through this lesson, Ms. Jarriel shows the students how the process of revision can involve adding both detail and voice.

Once the group has a significant piece of text to work with, it moves on to the next stage of the lesson, to discuss feedback and revision. Together, the class develops an example of a suggestion for peer feedback. Students decide that the script can be enhanced if they show how Tough Boris is tough by saying he fought against other pirates. Next, the students offer peer feedback, including positive comments as well as suggestions, within Google Docs.

Each student needs significant prompting and guidance as he or she begins revising *Tough Boris*. Students rely on the illustrations in the story to gain an understanding of the adjectives and to think of a realistic response for Tough Boris's dialogue. At first, Aiden creates dialogue that simply restates what the adjective means. Ms. Jarriel scaffolds his understanding by saying, "I want you to show me and not tell me." She asks him, "What scares you?" to connect him to familiar experiences. Once he has an understanding of context, he has an easier time creating dialogue. This also helps Aiden give peer feedback. He comments in the Google Docs file to offer the suggestion to "show how long the beard was." This feedback helps his coauthor consider an appropriate simile and he revises the line to read, "I have the longest beard, as long as a canon" (see figure 6.1, page 62).

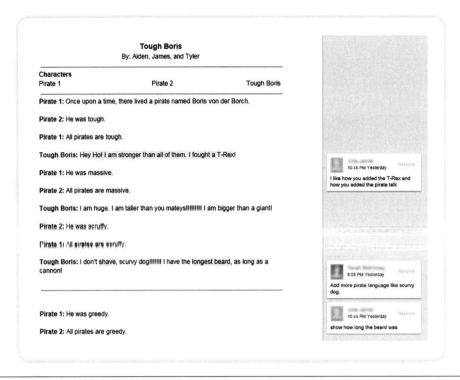

Figure 6.1: *Tough Boris* revisions after initial feedback.

After Tyler adds the detail, "Goodbye, old friend," a peer prompts him to think of what a pirate might say instead of "old friend." Based on feedback that he receives, Tyler changes "old friend" to "old matey," further enhancing the voice in the script. In fact, the dialogue helps the script to come alive (figure 6.2). As students continue to work, they read their peers' responses and make any changes as needed or suggested. The comment feature allows students to collaborate by sharing feedback. As a result, they engage in deeper reflection, revise their writing, and develop as writers.

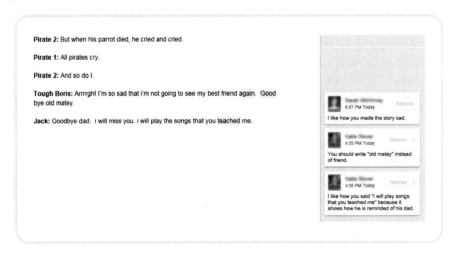

Figure 6.2: *Tough Boris* revisions showcasing deeper reflection about the text.

Understand Content Area Connections and Extended Applications

Google Docs can be utilized in the arts as well as physical education. Students can log musical practice hours and reflections, responding to prompts such as What did you practice today? and What do you need to work on tomorrow? In physical education, students could use the space to record how far they have run and what issues they have encountered along the way. For instance, a student training to run a 5K might record that she experienced shin pain on mile two of her three-mile run on Tuesday. Teachers can leave comments and suggestions to help students continue to grow.

Google Docs is a useful tool to help students collect and organize data in mathematics. For example, students choose a location from around the world and gather weather data for a specific period of time (for example, ten days). Students can explore websites such as the Weather Channel (www.weather.com) to collect and chart information, including the number of rainy days and sunny days, high daily temperatures, and low daily temperatures. They can compare changes in temperatures and wind gusts. Students can use a range of webcams located throughout the world to gain an understanding of an unfamiliar area as they collect data. For example, to compare the current weather conditions in Charlotte, North Carolina, to other cities around the world, students may visit websites such as WBTV HD Towercam (www.wbtv.com/category/273331/wbtv-tower-cam), EarthCam's Eiffel Tower Cam (www.earthcam.com/world/france/paris/?cam=eiffeltower_hd), and the Golden Gate Bridge in San Francisco (http://goo.gl/t5OTn3). As the students collect and record data, and gain an understanding of a geographic area, the students' teacher and peers can review the data and students' interpretive statements based on the data to offer feedback to inspire possible revision. Feedback sentence starters include:

- Your data seem to suggest . . .
- I like how you included . . .
- I wonder about . . . and . . .
- Have you thought about adding . . .

This project can grow in size and encompass cross-curricular goals. Teachers can encourage students to think about a place that they would like to visit. To plan accordingly, students would be required to gather data on weather conditions and tourist attractions. After collecting information over time, students could create a brochure or website on their area of interest.

Make Adaptations

There are times when an entire class or a small group of students may struggle to understand how to communicate with one another to provide formative feedback. If, after trying the sentence starters offered in this chapter, students continue to need additional scaffolding, the teacher may want to take advantage of Google Forms (www.google.com /forms) for students to first become proficient in providing self-reflective feedback.

The teacher can create a modified feedback form using the Google Drive (www.google .com/drive) applications. He or she can then provide students with a link to the form to complete. That information is automatically entered into a spreadsheet, making it convenient for the teacher. It is helpful to make the first item on the form a place where the student records his or her name. The next item might be a place for the student to write the title of the piece. For each form item, the teacher should use the drop-down menu next to Question Type to choose Text. For the next few prompt items, the teacher should probably choose Paragraph Text so that the students have more space to record their thoughts. Questions that the students may respond to include:

- What are you proud of in this piece? Please be specific.
- What do you need to work on: adding dialogue or details, narrowing focus, or something else? Please give an example from the text.
- Who is the audience for your piece? Why?
- If you had to summarize your piece in one sentence, what would that sentence be?
- Do you feel like you stay focused on the piece's purpose? Why or why not?
- What is your goal?
- What are your next steps?

The teacher can use the students' responses to these questions to help guide revision circles or individual conferences. Furthermore, if he or she notices a trend in the data, this information can help in crafting needed minilessons.

Reader's Theater Digital Movies

Ms. Kelley eagerly welcomes new students to the summer reading clinic at the university where she is pursuing her master's degree in literacy.

"James! I've been looking forward to meeting you! Today, we're going to do some reading and writing together. Can you tell me a little about yourself before we get started?"

With his head down, James simply shrugs his shoulders and murmurs that he doesn't really like to read or write. Attitudinal assessments and observations reveal that James demonstrates little interest in reading and writing and has difficulties with reading fluency. For instance, his reading is robotic as he reads word by word with little to no expression.

Additionally, James's parents shared his Individualized Education Plan to address his difficulties with attention deficit hyperactivity disorder (ADHD). This affects his ability to sit still and engage in reading or other learning activities for long periods of time. Equipped with his assessment data and her own experience as a classroom teacher, Ms. Kelley knows it is likely that his comprehension is affected as a result. She is determined to find engaging and meaningful methods to foster James's motivation while improving his overall reading and writing abilities.

The National Reading Panel (2000) states, "If text is read in a laborious and inefficient manner, it will be difficult for the child to remember what has been read and to relate the ideas expressed in the text to his or her background knowledge" (p. 11). Fluency is the bridge between decoding and comprehension. In other words, in order to fully understand what is being read, it is essential that students read fluently.

Like Ms. Kelley, many teachers are acutely aware of fluency's importance in developing students' reading comprehension skills. However, they may struggle to engage students in exercises that build fluency. In this chapter, we describe the use of iMovie as a way to engage students in reading as well as foster self-reflection and goal setting to improve reading fluency.

Learn the Benefits of Using Digital Tools to Improve Fluency

Fluency, a major pillar of effective reading, comprises several important components, including speed, accuracy, and prosody. Speed and accuracy are respectively defined as the rate at which the student reads and how many words are read correctly. Prosody is commonly referred to as *reading with expression* and *appropriate phrasing*. An overemphasis on reading for speed, since the emphasis of fluency became popular with the release of the National Reading Panel report in 2000, has created a misconception for many students that the best readers are the ones who read the fastest. As a result, the emphasis on reading for meaning has been overlooked. Furthermore, struggling readers often put so much cognitive energy into decoding the printed text that little energy is left for the meaning-making process. It is common for struggling readers to read in a slow and laborious manner, making comprehension of text nearly impossible (Chard, Vaughn, & Tyler, 2002). Additionally, students who have limited expression during oral reading are more likely to have poor comprehension during silent reading (Young & Rasinski, 2009).

Reader's theater is an authentic way to foster repeated readings while motivating reluctant readers (Chard et al., 2002). Using reader's theater creates opportunities for repeated readings with focus on speed, accuracy, and prosody since the script is usually read for a real audience. In reader's theater, students read their scripts with expression to help convey the text's meaning. Research reveals that the use of repeated readings leads to improved fluency for both the familiar text as well as new texts (Young & Rasinski, 2009). Reader's theater has demonstrated improved reading performance and overall engagement in reading (Griffith & Rasinski, 2004; Martinez, Roser, & Strecker, 1998/1999).

Although traditional practices of developing fluency through repeated readings and reader's theaters are still relevant, using digital tools provides students with a more authentic way to share their performances with a wider audience beyond those who are present for the live performance. Recorded performances can be shared with family members near and far as well as the general public using sites such as YouTube. Furthermore, recorded performances can be used as a tool for the readers to examine and evaluate their own performances.

Access Tools to Create Characters, Scripts, and Productions for Reader's Theater

Reader's theater has numerous benefits for students, including increased fluency and comprehension through more authentic repeated reading experiences. Students participate in repeated readings of familiar text to prepare for the reader's theater performance for a real audience. iMovie or other video software, such as Movie Maker or Splice (a popular mobile app), can be used as a self-evaluative tool during this process to enhance students' overall reading and performance (table 7.1, page 67).

Table 7.1: Digital Tools for Reader's Theater

Tool and URL	QR Code	Description
iMovie www.apple.com/mac/imovie		iMovie video editing software can be used to bring learning to life in the classroom. Users create and edit videos using Mac, iPhone, iPad, or iPod Touch. Music, titles, themes, and effects can be added to still images and videos.
Movie Maker https://support.microsoft.com/en-us/help/14220/windows-movie-maker-download		Movie Maker software for Windows allows users to create and edit a movie by downloading photos, video, and music into a storyboard. Each media type can easily be moved within the video by clicking and dragging to the appropriate place in the movie timeline. Visit www.readwritethink.org/files/resources/printouts/Using_Movie_Maker.pdf to read the useful manual "Using Windows Movie Maker."
ReadWriteThink Digital Comic Creator www.readwritethink.org/files/resources/interactives/comic		This free online tool allows students to create characters and backdrops when creating storyboards.
Dr. Chase Young's Alphabetical Listing of Readers Theater Scripts With Number of Parts www.thebestclass.org/rtscripts.html		This website offers access to free reader's theater scripts.

In this capacity, students use iMovie to record and critique each repeated reading experience. After reading the script, the students stop recording and collaboratively watch the video to discuss and reflect on their performance. With initial teacher prompting and modeling of self-reflective questioning, students begin to analyze their reading and their performance. Students discuss their responses to questions such as How was our reading?, Did we read with expression?, How could we improve our reading during the next read?, and How can we enhance our performance overall?

In addition to fostering student self-reflection about their reading, using video software such as iMovie exposes students to a range of technology skills. From simply learning about the digital tool and the logistics of how to use it to record, stop, watch, and rerecord, students can also learn useful skills such as video editing. For instance, when students record their last reader's theater performance, they can edit it to include music and text. Inserting the text as closed caption provides the viewer with an additional opportunity to read (Mraz & Rasinski, 2007). Through this final publication stage of the video, students can upload the video to YouTube or Vimeo and share the link with a wider audience.

Tablets such as iPads are useful digital tools to incorporate with reader's theater to take photos to use as backdrops for the performance. Students can either do an Internet search to find photos on the web or upload their own images that coordinate with the setting for their script. In doing so, students develop increased ownership over the reader's theater experience while continually being exposed to technology skills.

Transition to Reader's Theater Using Digital Tools

Whether students perform a published script or write their own, there are many ways to utilize reader's theater. Begin by giving students the opportunity to read and per-

form reader's theater scripts before they attempt to write their own scripts. Many examples of free reader's theater scripts can be found on websites such as Dr. Chase Young's Alphabetical Listing of Readers Theater Scripts (www.thebestclass.org/rtscripts.html). It is also useful for students to have access to the prewritten scripts to reference as examples while writing their own scripts.

After numerous opportunities to read and perform reader's theater, students can write their own scripts. Using previously read reader's theater scripts as mentor texts, students begin drafting. Comic strips or storyboards are effective tools to facilitate the planning process. Students can draw their characters and include dialogue using speech bubbles. An additional option is to use ReadWriteThink's digital comic creator. With this free online tool, students can select characters and backdrops from several options. Students can reference the comic creator or other graphic organizer when drafting their actual reader's theater scripts. A shared writing experience between both the teacher and the students is helpful for collaborative composition of the script. In this manner, the teacher offers scaffolding and support while eliciting input from students.

With at least one shared writing experience between the teacher and the students, teachers can gradually release students to work in small groups to create their own scripts throughout the school year. After drafting, students collaboratively read and revise their work. Students are typically quite excited at this point and will often ask if they can have a friend, parent, or teacher read the script. Encourage this! The more that the students realize the power of collaboration, the better off they will be.

When the students are satisfied with the script and are ready to publish, the teacher makes copies of the script for the group. The students should have multiple opportunities to collaboratively read, reread, and reread again. Since the purpose of the activity is authentic repeated readings to enhance reading fluency, students should have access to the script and therefore do not need to memorize the words. Continuous rereading helps improve students' accuracy, prosody, and rate. Consequently, students' fluency levels improve as they become more familiar with the script and they feel more comfortable with the script with each rereading.

As the students gain confidence with the script, they become ready to perform. The teacher and students can collectively determine a performance date. This helps with goal setting and inviting parents and other community members to attend. Students can also simply perform their reader's theater for their peers or another class in the school. When the students are ready to perform, they can head up to the front of the room (or to the stage) with their scripts in hand. They should project their voices, make eye contact with the audience, and have fun. There are no props or backdrops required for reader's theater. However, students can utilize PowerPoint and a Promethean whiteboard to display self-selected photographs, either taken with a tablet device or found on the web, as the backdrop.

Observe Digital Reader's Theater Tools in Action

To engage students in more meaningful repeated-reading experiences that also incorporate movement and more active participation to accommodate James's ADHD, Ms. Kelley introduces reader's theater as an instructional strategy. As part of her graduate studies, Ms. Kelley works with six struggling learners who participate in the university's Literacy Corner reading clinic for additional support in reading and writing. Students attend for one hour, four days a week for the month of June. Ms. Kelley and her peers, who are graduate students pursuing their master's degree in literacy education, provide intensive one-on-one and small-group instruction. After conducting a range of assessments, the graduate students learn that most of the students struggle with fluent reading. Many, like James, still read in a halting, robotic fashion with little to no expression. Therefore, the objective is to engage students in meaningful reading experiences that improve their fluency.

After Ms. Kelley divides the students into two groups based on their ability levels and personalities, the first group selects a reader's theater script based on a story from the book *The Stinky Cheese Man and Other Fairly Stupid Tales* by Jon Scieszka (1992). In advance of introducing the reader's theater script, Ms. Kelley dedicates several minilessons to teaching fluency. In this manner, Ms. Kelley reads a few short stories from *The Stinky Cheese Man* to model fluent reading. Before reading, she asks the students to evaluate her reading. She begins by reading slowly like a robot and then reads too quickly as a speed reader. After reading, she asks students to comment on the way she read. They enthusiastically exclaim that she reads too fast and too slow. The teacher discusses the importance of reading just right—like Goldilocks—with a proper pace and diction like we talk.

Ms. Kelley introduces the reader's theater script and the students are eager to select their roles. Once they determine roles, the group reads through the script with teacher support.

After discussing some of the unfamiliar vocabulary, such as *pungent*, the group practices reading the script multiple times independently, as a group, and at home for practice. Some students who demonstrate little interest in reading at home leave enthusiastically to practice their parts with their families.

After several opportunities to practice, Ms. Kelley adapts the *tape, check, chart* strategy (Allington, 2012) to include video analysis of the performance. This adaptation of repeated readings includes audio recordings of readings where students listen and mark their miscues. Students chart their progress and begin to reduce the number of miscues while increasing fluency after multiple readings and recordings of the same text (Allington, 2012).

Using iMovie to video record their skit, students are able to collaboratively view and evaluate their reading performance. Immediately after the performance, the students love watching themselves on the computer. To add an element of fun to this activity, the students watch the video with the purpose of self-evaluating their reading and performance of the reader's theater script. With guidance from Ms. Kelley, the students discuss ways to change their expression when reading, when to slow down or speed up as well as various movements to add to their script. This process leads to several revisions of the reader's theater script itself, including word changes, development of the ending, and correction of errors. Students make the necessary changes and practice again after reflecting. The group uses this technique multiple times before publishing its final iMovie and posting it to YouTube. Each time the students record their reader's theater script using iMovie, they notice improvements in their own reading as well as their peers' reading. Students learn to effectively collaborate, share feedback, and work together to enhance their performance. As a result, they are more confident with their reading and their fluency improves.

On the last day of the Literacy Corner, the students share their final iMovie with their families and other students. The audience is fully engaged, laughing at the funny parts and smiling ear to ear. They share the link to their movie with parents, who are then able to share the performance with family and friends.

Ms. Kelley's second group of students follows a slightly different process in creating and performing its reader's theater script. They retell a familiar text and use it to create a text reformulation (Beers, 2003) to integrate the reading and writing process. A text reformulation involves transforming an original text into a new text type. For instance, students can rewrite a chapter from a textbook in an ABC book structure. This strategy helps readers actively engage with text and think more critically about the reading (Beers, 2003). Ms. Kelley explains to the students that they will retell a familiar story and then write it in the format of a reader's theater that will later be performed; this demonstrates the fluency instructional objective.

After reading the book *How I Became a Pirate* by Melinda Long (2003), Ms. Kelley leads the students in a discussion of the story elements and encourages them to retell the story while she records the information on the projection screen. After reviewing story elements, the students collaborate to create a comic strip to retell the text's events.

The multiple retellings in oral, written list, and comic strip formats provide the students with opportunities to revisit text and familiarize themselves with the story structure. As students draw their comics, Ms. Kelley encourages them to consider what Jeremy Jacobs, the main character, might say when he sees the pirate ship. She discusses the role of dialogue between characters and how punctuation tells the reader how to read the text with expression. This provides a foundation for the project's next stage: students collaborate, with Ms. Kelley's support, to create a text reformulation of the story in a reader's theater.

Before transcribing the reader's theater script, Ms. Kelley shows students an example of a reader's theater other students perform on YouTube. She reminds students that reader's theater involves reading the script as opposed to memorizing the story. Next, using Microsoft Word on the projection screen, she engages students in a shared writing experience where she transcribes their ideas. They begin by listing the characters: Jeremy Jacobs, Braid Beard, the pirate crew, and the narrator. Projecting the writing for all students to see provides them with an opportunity to stop and reread so they can determine what to write next.

Shortly after the drafting process begins, the group decides to shift the focus of its retelling of *How I Became a Pirate*. To reflect their experience at the summer clinic, the students decide to change the setting of their reader's theater script from the beach where Jeremy Jacobs saw Braid Beard's pirate ship to the university library where the Literacy Corner is held. Then, the students decide the book's focus should be on learning to read since the story is occurring at the Literacy Corner.

The students decide that Jeremy Jacobs can teach Braid Beard and his crew how to read since in Melinda Long's version, the pirates didn't know how to read Jeremy Jacobs a bedtime story. This presents students with a great opportunity to revisit effective reading strategies they are learning about and applying to their own reading-skills development. The students decide that the story's theme should convey that reading is a treasure that can take you on adventures.

After discussing options, the students elect to do a live performance instead of videotaping an iMovie. However, they incorporate technology in another way. Since this group rewrites a familiar story and changes the setting to the Literacy Corner, it decides it will be more authentic if the members use images of their surroundings to display on the projection screen as a backdrop for their reader's theater performance. The students use the iPad to take photos of different areas of the library and also use the Google Images (https://images.google.com) search feature to find photos of the lake behind campus to use in the beginning of the script. They list settings including the library, the lake where the pirate ship came ashore, the computer to search for books, and the children's section. They save and insert the images into a PowerPoint file to use during the performance. Having students take photos to use as the backdrop increases their sense of ownership in the production. Additionally, sequencing the photos correctly in the PowerPoint gives yet another opportunity to practice retelling their script. With these opportunities to spend time reading in meaningful ways, students increase their engagement with the text, and as Guthrie and Wigfield (2000) note, "engaged reading is strongly associated with reading achievement" (p. 404).

Understand Content Area Connections and Extended Applications

Reader's theater and similar adaptations are great ways to bring social studies curriculum to life. Many teachers incorporate a wax museum as a way for students to take on the persona of various historical figures. They begin by selecting an individual from a particular time period they are studying. Next, students conduct research to learn about the person's life and his or her contributions or significance. To demonstrate their understanding and teach others, students dress up as the historical figure and then present information from the figure's perspective when visitors approach them in the wax museum. Students can create short videos of themselves dressed as the historical figure and record relevant information to digitize this concept. They can post QR codes around the classroom or the school for other students to watch long after the wax museum closes.

Additionally, reader's theater can help students strengthen their content knowledge by imagining the perspectives of other historical periods or other cultures. Students can collaboratively create and perform a script to reenact important historical events as key historical figures. This approach deepens students' understanding of the historical figures as they consider how individuals interacted and how those conversations impacted various events during the time period. Students might also develop current events into a reader's theater to tell the news from around the world. To provide a context for the reenacted historical or current events, students can find photographs of historical documents or figures or places featured in current events by using a Google Images search. Then, students can use the images as the backdrop on a projection screen when they perform their reader's theater script.

Make Adaptations

For students who may seem introverted or nervous about performing a reader's theater script for a live audience, it might be helpful to give them opportunities to practice by individually recording themselves reading. This allows the student to self-evaluate and make any necessary changes before participating in the group session. The repeated readings through the recordings can enhance the student's confidence before participating in group practice sessions. Furthermore, this same approach can be used for the group readings. By engaging in ongoing conversations within the group, students learn how to provide their peers with appropriate feedback to foster growth and improvement before performing the script. Through these individual and group opportunities for reflection and evaluation, participants develop a sense of confidence while improving their reading abilities.

PART III

Tools to Facilitate Performance and Publication

Informational Writing Using Infographics

Students are excited as they walk into Ms. Gault's fourth-grade classroom. As part of their integrated science unit on plants, they spent the previous week reading and learning about trees. To address language arts standards, Ms. Gault's students compare the perspectives of loggers and environmentalists. Ms. Gault models how to read with a purpose to select key information that supports the particular perspective being examined. Today, they will create infographics to highlight what they learned about trees, from the perspectives of both loggers and environmentalists. Ready to begin work, students gather their iPads and form groups.

As Ms. Gault walks around the room, she hears echoes of distress.

"It won't load!" Allie shouts.

"My information won't save," Amira adds.

The website isn't functioning on their iPads. Ms. Gault quickly monitors and adjusts her plan. Instead of having students begin work on the tablets, she has them plan on paper. Students gather materials and collaboratively create their plans as paper blueprints that they will take with them when they get on the computers. While working on their blueprints, students refer to the texts and discuss their ideas as they consider evidence to support both the loggers' and environmentalists' perspectives on trees. Students choose the most salient information to include on the infographics.

While working on their blueprint, Amira tells Allie, "I didn't realize that loggers cut down trees for a reason. We use that wood to make furniture, homes, and even paper."

"Yeah, but the environmentalists are trying to keep trees from getting cut down for a reason, too. We need the trees so that we can have clean air and animals have their homes. I wonder if there is a way to cut down fewer trees but also let loggers keep their jobs," Allie ponders aloud.

With blueprints in hand, students head to the computers to create their infographics.

Analyzing information, comparing sources, and sharing findings are essential components of demonstrating knowledge. As Ms. Gault's fourth graders discover, competing viewpoints often have equally valid supporting evidence. Infographics are one way students can compare and contrast multiple positions on issues as well as share the significance of what they learn. In this chapter, we explore digital infographic tools that help students to synthesize information and enhance content knowledge.

Learn the Benefits of Using Digital Infographics to Enhance Content Knowledge

Consider the last time you learned new information from reading. Do you envision yourself with a pen in hand? Did you take notes or write about the topic before, during, or after you were reading, listening, or viewing to deepen understanding? Perry D. Klein and Amy Meichi Yu (2013) describe writing to learn as "an educational practice in which teachers assign students writing with the intention of helping them to understand subject matter in disciplines such as science, social studies, history, English, and mathematics" (p. 166).

Not only does writing help students summarize, make connections, and enhance comprehension, it can also serve as a formative assessment. In fact, that information provides the teacher with an idea of what students currently understand and what misconceptions, if any, exist (Harvey & Goudvis, 2007; Knipper & Duggan, 2006). Students require additional cognitive energy to write about a topic rather than to only read about it (Shanahan, 2013). Consequently, students deepen their understanding of the content they are exploring. Writing to learn requires active engagement rather than a passive approach to learning (Knipper & Duggan, 2006). Yet, writing to enhance learning does not necessarily need to be a complex task. For example, students might record thoughts on sticky notes or in a book's margins as a way to think through their thoughts and ideas (Harvey & Goudvis, 2007) for a more comprehensive learning experience (Shanahan, 2013).

While writing to learn can be an individual, solitary act in early stages, it does not need to be an isolated experience. In fact, students can write about informational texts for various audiences, thereby establishing a sense of authorship (Newell, VanDerHeide, & Wilson, 2013). Most curriculum standards require that students write informational texts for diverse audiences. Specifically, Common Core ELA anchor standard two for writing states that students "write informative/explanatory texts to examine and convey complex ideas and information clearly and accurately through the effective selection, organization, and analysis of content" (CCRA.W.2, NGA & CCSSO, 2010). Anchor standard four for writing takes into consideration authors' audiences by requiring students to "produce clear and coherent writing in which the development, organization, and style are appropriate to task, purpose, and audience" (CCRA.W.4, NGA & CCSSO, 2010).

Digital spaces and tools expand the ways students write, as well as the audiences with whom they share their writing. Traditionally, when students engage in writing-to-learn practices, they take notes with paper and pen to present their findings to the teacher. When making presentations, they often stand next to trifold poster boards and orally present information with the audience physically present. With the influx of digital tools, students can present new information in multimodal digital formats and expand their audience. For example, they may write or transfer notes to a digital space where they can share and create notes collaboratively. An additional benefit of using digital tools for writing is that students can hyperlink supplementary materials in their digital documents. Students can also discuss their learning with an authentic audience beyond the teacher, sharing their learning with interested parties across the globe. A digital approach allows students to share their learning with a wider audience over and over again and access their presentations easily. In this way, the students become experts on the topic.

Access Tools to Engage Students in Analyzing Texts, Sharing Information, and Collaborating with Peers

Infographics, short for information graphics, are fun and a fairly simple way to format and share information. Table 8.1 provides an overview of some of the most useful digital infographic tools for classrooms. Several of these quite popular and user-friendly sites allow the user to create infographics for free.

Table 8.1: Digital Tools Creating Infographics and Making Content Area Connections

Tool and URL	QR Code	Description
Canva www.canva.com		Canva has a wealth of templates, images, filters, fonts, and shapes. Canva can be used on the web or an iPad.
Infogr.am's Learn by Numbers https://infogr.am/education		Infogr.am's focus on charts and graphs makes it especially suitable for math and science.
Smore www.smore.com		Once a user chooses a free template, he or she can insert components such as audio, text, pictures, forms, and galleries and type information into the infographic, sometimes described as a digital flyer or newsletter.

continued →

Piktochart http://piktochart.com		Piktochart has a free option as well as a pro option for educators. While both accounts allow PDF exports, only the pro account has high-resolution images.
Easel.ly www.easel.ly		Easel.ly offers several templates and images to help students and teachers create graphics.
National Geographic Education's Encyclopedia Entry for *pollution* http://education.nationalgeographic.com/education/encyclopedia/pollution/?ar_a=1		This website includes student-friendly information about pollution.
Climate Kids: NASA's Eyes on the Earth http://climatekids.nasa.gov/menu/big-questions		This website provides student-friendly information about climate change.

While we'll explore National Geographic Education's encyclopedia entry page on *pollution* and Climate Kids: NASA's Eyes on the Earth site about global climate change later in the chapter, let's turn to three especially classroom-friendly sites: (1) Smore, (2) Piktochart, and (3) Easel.ly.

1. **Smore** offers free templates and is simple to navigate. While an email address is necessary, it takes less than a minute to sign up for an account. Once a user chooses a template, he or she can insert components such as audio, text, pictures, forms, and video and immediately begin typing information into the infographic, sometimes described as a digital flyer or newsletter. Smore allows the creator access to analytics about his or her infographics. The creator can see such information as where readers are geographically located, how many times people have clicked on links, and how many times people have scrolled and read to the end of the infographic. These statistics can help students establish a sense of authorship and a sense of connection to their audience. They can visually understand the scope of their words by seeing how varied their audience is.

2. **Piktochart** has a free option as well as a pro option for educators. The free option has limited templates and image uploads. Additionally, the Piktochart watermark is present with a free account. A pro account offers users the option to restrict who can see a published infographic. While both the pro and free accounts allow for PDF exports, only the pro account has high-resolution images. After deciding on the type of account, the user can

select a template. Then, the user can double click on any of the blocks to add unique text or images and change the background, colors, and lines in the template.

3. **Easel.ly** offers several available templates and images. Users may select a premade template or upload their own background image. Additionally, users may add text and images to the template at any time. They may save changes and create, revise, and edit the infographic over a period of time. When the user is finished, he or she may share a link to the infographic or download and print a PDF. Many teachers and students find Easel.ly easy to use. In fact, Easel.ly won a Best Websites for Teaching and Learning 2013 award from the American Association for School Librarians (Easel.ly, 2014).

Now, let's look more in depth at how easy it is to transition from sharing information in traditional formats to using Easel.ly to facilitate creating and presenting information in digital spaces.

Transition to Representing and Sharing Content Knowledge Using Easel.ly

As with the implementation of most technological tools, it is helpful for the teacher to understand the infographic before asking students to create one. To begin his or her infographic, the teacher can use notes he or she already prepared for the unit topic or lesson. For example, an educator preparing to teach students about point of view might gather first-, second-, and third-person point of view definitions, images, and examples. Having that information readily available allows the teacher to devote all time and attention to becoming familiar with the online infographic's features. Once the teacher creates the sample infographic, it can be displayed digitally on a Smart Board or as print copies if no Smart Board is available. Additionally, teachers can supply students with the hyperlink to the infographic for further study and review outside of the classroom. Easel.ly also provides the opportunity to download a PDF of the infographic, so if a student does not have access to the Internet at home, the teacher can still provide him or her with a paper copy.

Though the process of creating infographics is similar, we'll walk users through the steps to create an infographic on Easel.ly. Visit Easel.ly (www.easel.ly) to register for an account. To do so, provide your email address and choose a password. Once registered, select the Start Fresh tile to begin with an empty slate, or choose an editable Public Visual infographic. If starting fresh, the next step is to select a *vheme* (visual theme) template. The free version of Easel.ly permits a user to choose from a limited number of templates; however, upgrading to the pro account allows the user to access all the templates.

Available vhemes often include text. Therefore, once a user selects a vheme, he or she must erase the sample text and images before adding new text or images. Additionally, users can change the font and font size by highlighting the text and using the drop-down menu to select another font or size. To delete text, images, or a combination of both, click on the text or image and then click on the trash can icon in the upper-left corner. To delete large portions of text, images, and so on, use the mouse to create a box around large groups of items and then click on the trash can.

After users delete any undesired text and images and choose the font and font size for their vhemes, they're ready to customize their infographics with text and images. To add text, click on the Text button at the top of the page. Select from title, header, or body text. Then click and drag that tile to any location in the infographic and begin typing. To insert images, select Objects and then choose a category from the drop-down menu for a wide selection of clip art–like images. Click on the image and drag it anywhere on the infographic. Users may change the size and rotation of objects by clicking on the top of the image and then waiting for boxes to appear. Click on the boxes around the sides of the object to change its size. To change its rotation, click on the top of the image and wait for a plus sign to appear. Then, drag the plus sign to change the object's rotation.

When ready to view the finished product, click Present. To go back and continue editing, press Exit. At any point, the user can name and save the infographic by clicking Save in the upper-left corner. Users may share their infographics privately or publicly by providing a link to the work. A further option is to download a PDF of the infographic.

In the next section, we check in with Ms. Gault's fourth-grade class to see how using digital tools to create infographics improved students' content knowledge, collaboration with peers, and writing skills.

Observe Easel.ly in Action

Ms. Gault wants her fourth-grade students to practice their informational writing skills and to convey complex ideas clearly for their audience by creating infographics that highlight different perspectives of loggers and environmentalists. After reading and rereading informational texts on the topic of loggers and environmentalists, students gather, process, and synthesize key information. Then, they work on phrasing and create blueprints to share their findings. The blueprints serve as traditional rough drafts that will eventually become students' infographics. In this collaborative activity, students refer to the informational texts to check facts or record specific figures. Giving students time to carefully think through and determine the information, figure placement, and colors for their infographics allows them to deeply consider and reflect on the texts they read.

After gathering information from both the loggers' and the environmentalists' perspectives, deciding on the layout, and proofreading their work, students begin creating their infographics using Easel.ly. Ms. Gault circulates throughout the room and answers any questions that her students have about the technology. Students help one another with using the site. In fact, when most students encounter roadblocks, they attempt to troubleshoot the issue on their own before consulting with Ms. Gault. Not only does students' content knowledge expand, but their understanding of technology and how to use digital tools to further their learning increases as well.

As evidenced by students' infographics, active engagement in reading, writing, creating, collaborating, and sharing led students to a deeper understanding of the environmental issues surrounding trees. It was obvious that the students worked hard on their infographics. They remained focused throughout the project and their finished infographics contained rich information, detailing the viewpoints of both the loggers and the environmentalists. Judging by their engagement and finished infographics, students not only enjoyed using informational texts to create infographics in Ms. Gault's classroom, they also learned the science content being studied.

Understand Content Area Connections and Extended Applications

Often, there is not a significant focus on writing to learn in the content areas since most teachers spend the bulk of their writing time working on the nuances of process writing (Knipper & Duggan, 2006). However, finding the time to teach students methods to help them as they write to learn is important. Writing is an effective way to increase students' comprehension across the content areas (Knipper & Duggan, 2006). Not only do teachers focus on content at this time, they also equip students with skills to help them throughout their lives.

In social studies, students could use an infographic to convey their new knowledge about a given topic. For example, students studying World War II could compile images, information, and historical accounts from participants on Japanese internment camps. After reading poems, articles, digital texts, and stories such as *So Far From the Sea* (Bunting, 1998) and *Baseball Saved Us* (Mochizuki, 1993), students could approach the information from the children's, soldiers', parents', and outsiders' perspectives. The link to this infographic could be embedded in a class website, shared through email, or posted on the class blog so other students, parents, and individuals interested in World War II could view the information. This gives the student access to a much wider, more authentic audience than a one-dimensional poster presentation. Additionally, students will more likely be engaged in the content and put forth more effort as a result.

In science, when studying a topic such as pollution and its effects, an infographic would serve as a visual reminder of student learning. The National Geographic website's entry on *pollution* or NASA's Climate Kids site might be useful places for students to begin reading and collecting information. Once students have chosen an area of focus within the larger topic of pollution, they can photograph their own town to make the conversation about pollution more relevant. Upon completing their infographics, students can share their learning and use the infographics to educate students in earlier grades. The infographic might even be a starting point for real action. Students could share their infographics with various stakeholders connected with the concept to take steps to inspire change.

For example, after reading about a polluted river basin in their hometown, students learn that fertilized yards, pet waste, and new home construction all contribute to pollution. Students work together to create an infographic to share relevant information and then implore their town's citizens to stop fertilizing their yards and to start picking up and properly disposing of pet waste. By sharing their learning with the community, students hope to impact positive change.

Mathematics easily lends itself to this technology with the use of graphs, charts, and images. Students could demonstrate step by step how to solve a word problem on an infographic. Having to think through the process and explain in writing can help deepen students' understanding of the mathematical concept (McCormick, 2010).

Make Adaptations

Asking students to read multiple sources, including both print and digital texts, to find relevant information and create infographics may prove to be overwhelming. To combat this issue, students should have a clear purpose for their infographics, as the students in Ms. Gault's class did. A research template is useful to facilitate this process (see the appendix, page 148).

Breaking a task into manageable chunks is a way to help keep students from feeling overwhelmed. Giving students an agenda helps them maintain focus. A possible schedule might be:

Day 1: Read, read, read!

Day 2: Conduct research, gather notes (refer to the research template).

Day 3: Continue conducting research.

Day 4: Begin constructing blueprint.

Day 5: Continue work on blueprint.

Day 6: Begin infographic (select template and write headings and subheadings).

Day 7: Finish infographic.

As students progress through the year, the schedule and research template might prove unnecessary. There may also be several students who continue to need the extra scaffolding for the duration of the year. As with anything, differentiation is central. See figure 8.1 (page 83) for a sample checklist.

In order to better individualize instruction for students conducting research for their infographics, the teacher can confer with each student or group of students. Additionally, the teacher may want to have students take a few minutes to reflect on their progress at the end of each period. They can answer questions such as How did it go today? and What is your plan for tomorrow? The teacher can quickly read through each response as students transition to another activity. Reading the responses may help the teacher determine which student to meet with first in the coming days. Guiding students through the research process can be cumbersome. However, infographics can make a difference. Encouraging students to share their research on an infographic provides an authentic reason for students to conduct the research in the first place, leads to more engaged learning, and may contribute to making a difference in the community.

Day	Task	Check When Complete	Date Completed
1	Read, read, read!		
2	Conduct research, gather notes (refer to the research template).		
3	Continue conducting research.		
4	Begin constructing blueprint.		
5	Continue work on blueprint.		
6	Begin infographic (select template and write headings and subheadings).		
7	Finish infographic.		

Figure 8.1: Student checklist.

*Visit **go.SolutionTree.com/technology** for a free reproducible version of this figure.*

Collaborative Digital Story Retelling

Upon hearing that it is story time, Mrs. McKinney's kindergarten students skip to the carpet area with excitement. The students listen intently as Mrs. McKinney reads them some of their favorite stories during their study of different versions of the traditional tale of The Gingerbread Man. They love to talk with their peers about their favorite parts of stories, character traits, and connections to texts they previously read. Yet, when Mrs. McKinney asks her students to retell a story after she read it to them, they sit quietly with blank stares. Instantly, she realizes they need modeling, support, and practice in order to feel comfortable with the task of retelling familiar stories.

As she reflects, Mrs. McKinney realizes that a possible challenge for her students might be that upon finishing the book, it was closed and placed on an easel. Therefore, students only saw the cover, without access to the pages of the book. Knowing that her students love to participate in picture walks before the reading of a story, Mrs. McKinney wonders if, after reading, it might also be helpful to do a picture walk of sorts to refresh students' memories of the story events and characters.

Mrs. McKinney considers creating felt puppets for students to recreate the story and then remembers an app that allows students to create digital puppets. Aware of how much her students love using technology, Mrs. McKinney instantly knows this is a way to engage students in the reading and retelling experience. During story time the next day, Mrs. McKinney introduces her students to the Puppet Pals app to foster collaboration and retelling in an engaging and innovative way.

Reading aloud is a common practice in early childhood and elementary classrooms used to promote language and literacy development. Interactive read-alouds provide a forum for students to actively engage with their teacher and peers to discuss texts and deepen their understanding. According to Lev Vygotsky's (1978) work, the construction of meaning is dependent on social interaction. Therefore, opportunities for scaffolded discussion and collaboration are essential for students to create understanding.

But sometimes, like Mrs. McKinney, teachers need a little help to engage students in discussion and collaboration. This chapter presents the Puppet Pals app as a way to foster digital storytelling skills with even the youngest students.

Learn the Benefits of Using Digital Tools for Reading Aloud and Story Retelling

Through discussions about literature, students learn valuable lessons about working together to communicate effectively. Karen D. Wood, Nancy L. Roser, and Miriam Martinez (2001) find that students need to collaborate in order to cooperate or get along with others. They suggest the use of collaborative discussion around a commonly read text as a springboard to deepen socially constructed meaning. Jessica L. Hoffman (2011) describes how a kindergarten class redesigned instruction for the classroom read-aloud to incorporate more interactive discussion focused on interpretive meaning and demonstrated the possibility for higher-level literacy instruction. According to Hoffman (2011), "Children are entirely capable of engaging in higher level literacy practices when their meaning making is facilitated by teacher supports and interactive discussion" (p. 184).

After engaging in interactive read-alouds, teachers can encourage young learners to retell the story to foster oral language, comprehension, and sense of story structure. Retelling is a generative task that involves engagement in active discussion as well as a role in text assimilation and reconstruction (Morrow, 1996). Teachers can gauge students' comprehension through retelling as they observe the "student's thought processes, what the child values as important and cultural influences in story interpretation" (McKenna & Stahl, 2009, p. 168).

Similar to traditional retellings where readers engage in performative response by manipulating text with props such as flannel boards and hand, stick, or finger puppets to create meaning (Sipe, 2008), apps such as Puppet Pals can be used to retell familiar stories in digital spaces. The advent of the digital age continues to expand definitions of literacy (Leu, 2000). Therefore, young students must be equipped with skills needed to use technology to communicate, create, and collaborate in our technology-focused society. In this age of digital tools and multiliteracies, there are increasing demands for students to collaborate in order to consume and produce multimodal texts in online spaces. Digital storytelling addresses these needs and provides many benefits to students. For instance, it gives students the ability to record their oral retelling and enables them to listen to themselves and others, which promotes oral language skills development. Furthermore, online storytelling allows users to share their versions of the retelling with others time and time again.

Access Digital Tools That Promote Students' Oral Language and Storytelling Skills

Digital storytelling tools help students develop oral-language skills, comprehension, and sense of story in fun, engaging ways, and it helps teachers assess students' abilities to communicate their understanding. Table 9.1 highlights Puppet Pals, Scribble Press, and Educreations apps that are especially well suited to classroom read-alouds and story retelling. These interactive apps allow users to engage in meaningful ways as they respond to reading experiences. For instance, a feature of Puppet Pals includes photo-shopping characters and settings from any text through the camera app. Settings can be customized by uploading the images of the familiar text as a backdrop. Then, users take an image of a character from a recently read text, crop it, and manipulate it by moving it around the screen and recording their oral retelling or story from the character's perspective. Rather than photo-shopping these images, apps such as Educreations and Scribble Press allow users to draw, color, and insert images to create an artistic representation of information or, in this case, a reaction to or retelling of a familiar text.

Table 9.1: Digital Tools for Interactive Story Retelling

Site and URL	QR Code	Description
Puppet Pals (Director's Pass Version) https://itunes.apple.com /us/app/puppet-pals-hda -directors-pass/id46213 4755?mt=8		Users can create narrative puppet shows through provided characters and settings or with student-created characters and settings, which can be created with the paid Director's Pass version of the app.
Scribble Press app http://app.scribblepress .com		Students can use personal photos or drawing tools to create characters.
Educreations www.educreations.com		Educreations records voice, drawing, and inserted images to produce a video presentation that can easily be shared online.

The Puppet Pals app allows users to create narrative puppet shows by providing characters and settings or with student-created characters and settings. The Director's Pass version offers several features including a wide range of characters, such as celebrities and politicians, as well as the ability to create an actor or backdrop from a photo, zoom in, rotation, and flip of characters. All shows can be saved, played at a later time, and exported to share with a wider audience on the Internet. Puppet Pals offers limitless opportunities for story creation, creativity, and collaboration. In fact, puppets can be simultaneously manipulated to allow students to work together to collaboratively tell the story. The app can be used to focus on identifying characters, setting, and major events from a fictional text and retelling the story using all those features. In primary grades classrooms, Puppet Pals fosters language development (Sandvick, Smørdal, & Østerud, 2012), sense of story, and collaboration.

Transition to Digital Retelling Using Puppet Pals

To begin using Puppet Pals in the classroom, first download the free or paid Director's Pass version. To introduce this app, begin by modeling how to retell a familiar read-aloud using prerecorded Puppet Pals presentations on the SMART Board. Once students have an opportunity to create a Puppet Pal retelling with teacher support, they can work with their peers in a small group to collaboratively retell a text they read during guided reading.

With the paid version, students can begin to create their own characters by tapping on the Add Actor From Photo option. Next, they select the image from saved photos (see figure 9.1). Students can use photos or create their own characters with drawing apps such as Scribble Press. With the character selected, the students then cut out the puppet for the stage, using their fingers to outline and trace the character. When finished, click Accept to add the new character. Students can select up to eight characters for their puppet show. These can be chosen from the provided characters or from student-created characters. Next, students will select the backgrounds for the puppet show (see figure 9.2, page 89). Use a similar process as described in character creation and select up to five backgrounds. Students can edit backgrounds by moving and zooming in on images. The order in which students select their backgrounds will be the order they appear on the creation slide represented by the tassels. After selecting characters and the setting within the app, or creating their own, students select the backdrop by tapping on the tassels at the top of the screen.

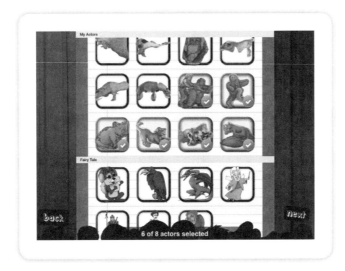

Source: Polished Play, 2016, with permission.

Figure 9.1: Select a Puppet Pal.

Source: Polished Play, 2016, with permission.

Figure 9.2: Select a background.

There are several acting options available when creating the puppet show. First, with a background setting selected, students can use two fingers to pinch and stretch characters to resize them on the screen. Double tap characters to rotate and flip them. When students are ready to record their stories, only the action inside the white box will be viewable. The space around the perimeter is similar to being in the wings of the stage, where characters wait for their part to appear. Multiple characters can be controlled at once, making it easy for students to collaborate through interactive storytelling. After practicing, students can record simply by tapping the record button. Then they touch the screen to select and manipulate the characters while recording their oral story or retelling. Teachers can pause the recording to allow students to change characters, setting, or simply to collect and organize their thoughts. When finished, click End to stop recording and click Save to name the production. This will save it within Puppet Pals; however, to share it outside of the app, students need to export their puppet show to the camera roll for later posting on websites.

Observe Puppet Pals in Action

During their author study of Jan Brett, Mrs. McKinney engages her kindergarteners in a retelling of the book *The Mitten* (Brett, 1989) using Puppet Pals. Before the lesson, Mrs. McKinney uses the Director's Pass paid version to take photos of the book's characters. She uses the cutting feature to trim the characters as needed. Additionally, she uses the iPad to take a photo of outside Baba's house for the backdrop. The actors and backdrop are stored within the app so that their whole-group time can focus on the actual retelling.

When it is time for the lesson, Mrs. McKinney's students eagerly gather to listen to the story. After reading the book, Mrs. McKinney announces that they will be using puppets to retell the story. However, these aren't just any ordinary puppets—these puppets are on the iPad. Her students clap and smile as the SMART Board displays the image of the Puppet Pals app. With the iPad connected to the docking station, students are ready to learn how to use digital puppets to retell a story.

During the first phase of the retelling, the kindergarteners recall the majority of characters from memory and use the text as a support when necessary. One by one the students approach the iPad and tap on an actor icon so that a green check mark will appear. The class counts the total number of checks and reviews the book to make sure they have selected all the characters. Next, the students quickly recognize Baba's house as the most appropriate setting for their retelling and a student selects the appropriate setting icon, displaying a green check.

The app displays the backdrop in the center of the screen, with all the selected actors scattered across the board. In order to help students with sequencing, Mrs. McKinney asks them to help her organize the characters and put them in an ordered line based on when they appear in the story. They work together to select the characters and place Nicki and Baba in the center of the stage with the remaining actors in order below the stage. With the characters ready, her class begins retelling the story.

Mrs. McKinney models retelling the beginning of the book in the early phases of introducing the Puppet Pals app. She begins the retelling: "Baba knitted Nicki some mittens and she told him to keep them safe as he went outside and played." As students become more comfortable and confident with retelling with their peers, she encourages them to participate in the retelling. The first student moves Nicki on the screen and records, "He climbed up the tree and lost his mitten." The next student moves the rabbit to the center of the stage and says, "The bunny comes along and finds the mitten." The retelling continues to be a collaborative experience as students retell small sections of the story by moving the appropriate characters and recording their voices.

The students continue and move the next five characters into a pile as they all climb into the mitten. As a whole class, the students record themselves saying, "The mouse climbs in and the bear went *achoo!*" The final student comes up to the iPad and records the ending: "Then Nicki came and got his mitten back. He went back and the grandma looked into the window and saw that he didn't lose his mitten." Once the retelling is complete, Mrs. McKinney saves their Puppet Pals recording so that it can be accessed within the app's Saved Shows feature. The students immediately beg to watch their video. They all smile and cheer as they celebrate creating their first collaborative retelling using Puppet Pals.

Recording retells using Puppet Pals gives Mrs. McKinney's students multiple opportunities to practice and develop their oral-language skills while collaborating with their peers. Throughout the process, students provide assistance and offer feedback to their classmates, especially to support students who are somewhat shy and hesitant with the retelling. If asked to retell the story independently, some of these young kindergarten students will be reluctant and have difficulty with the given task. Through collaboration with their peers, the opportunities for social interaction increase their comfort and confidence in oral retelling using the Puppet Pals app. The app makes the traditional reading and retelling experience more engaging for these emergent learners and offers enhanced oral-language opportunities.

Students also gain greater exposure to the use of various technology features like recording, tapping, and dragging items across the tablet screen and using a variety of customizable features within the app to practice story elements including determining appropriate setting, selecting main characters, and story sequencing. These skills will deepen students' overall comprehension.

Understand Content Area Connections and Extended Applications

Students can use Puppet Pals for their own narrative writing once they become familiar with the app. It can be used during all stages of the writing process, including prewriting, drafting, revising, editing, and publishing. In preparation, the teacher can upload photos of familiar places in the classroom and around the school, such as the playground, classroom centers, the cafeteria, related arts' rooms, and the bus stop, as background options to foster writing about school experiences. Students can also check out iPads to bring home and capture images of their communities and lives outside of school. This approach helps teachers develop a sense of students' *funds of knowledge* (Allen, 2007; Moll, Amanti, Neff, & Gonzalez, 1992). In other words, students come to school with bodies of cultural and cognitive resources and literacy practices that work within the communities they participate in (Moll et al., 1992). By examining students' funds of knowledge, educators deepen their understanding of students' lives and can make connections between students' lives at home and school. Axelrod (2014) describes how photography can be used to learn about students and minorities from historically marginalized communities. According to Axelrod (2014),

> By asking children to take pictures of their everyday lives, what they do after school, where they go grocery shopping, playgrounds, playmates, toys, food, chores, we can learn more about the children, their individual cultures, family and community dynamics, and experiences. (p. 52)

Technology use allows for increased access to capture and share images outside of the school's four walls. These images can then be uploaded as backgrounds in the Puppet Pals app so students can tell their own narrative stories.

Another option would be to have students create informational pieces to teach others about a shared experience, such as a place they visited during a field trip. Students can work in groups to take photos of highlights during a field trip. They can upload the images from their field trip and work together to teach others about the place and what they learned once they return to school. By creating a digital field trip with the Puppet Pals app, students offer access to a wider audience. For example, the teacher can inform her students that at next year's open house, this show will be played to incoming students and parents. What a way to get current students excited about showing off their knowledge!

Additionally, the teacher can highlight fun, upcoming field trips and technological applications in her classroom for the new students and parents. Each activity provides students with engaging ways to practice essential oral-language and storytelling skills.

Teachers can provide students with various options to demonstrate understanding in multiple content areas. This affords students with authentic opportunities to practice fluency and language skills while deepening content knowledge. For instance, rather than writing a paragraph about President Abraham Lincoln's role during the Civil War, students can use the Puppet Pals app to create a puppet skit to demonstrate their learning and teach others. When studying a unit in science, students may create a Puppet Pals narrative explaining a specific concept. For example, if a fifth-grade class is studying mixtures and solutions, students may begin by uploading related images. Next, they could create a character to explain that a mixture is a combination of two or more components while a solution is a type of mixture that cannot easily be separated and contains a solute as well as a solvent.

Make Adaptations

With its many manipulable features, Puppet Pals can be used in the classroom to meet the diverse needs of all students. For instance, students who benefit from hands-on learning are able to manipulate the characters and move them around the screen as they retell their stories. For verbal and auditory learners or students who struggle with writing, this app provides opportunities for oral storytelling. Puppet Pals fosters a process approach to oral composition. Students do not need to be fearful of making errors or doing perfect work. For instance, when one student in Mrs. McKinney's class stops and exclaims, "Oh no! I messed up!" Mrs. McKinney gently reminds her that she can easily press the *Back* button and do it again. The ease and flexibility of this digital tool allows students to have multiple opportunities to practice and interact with story retelling and composition experiences. In comparison with traditional writing, students can easily revise and make adjustments without tearing holes in the paper by erasing, leaving them feeling even more frustrated.

Additionally, since the Puppet Pals app fosters oral language and composition, it can be helpful for teachers to pair struggling writers or ELs with more confident writers. Language acquisition occurs through social interactions with both adults and peers. Collaborating with a writing buddy allows struggling writers and ELs to gain confidence and extend their reading and writing abilities. They can collaborate to brainstorm, plan, tell, and revise their stories. Oral language and literacy develop together, meaning that what students acquire from speaking and listening to others greatly influences their ability to read and write. Providing students with opportunities to develop oral language skills are critical, as students who fall behind in oral language and literacy development are less likely to be successful beginning readers (Strickland et al., 2004). The Puppet Pal app provides several opportunities throughout the instructional day to support ELs not only in literacy blocks, but also in the content areas.

Published Writing

The classroom is abuzz as Mrs. McKinney's kindergarteners gather on the colorful carpet in front of the SMART Board to share their published eBooks. They clap and cheer for their friends as they celebrate publishing their first books online. Mrs. McKinney scrolls down the class blog where the students' recorded readings of their eBooks are published to share the comment section with these young authors.

Their principal remarks, "I am so impressed with the books you are making. I would certainly love to see more books from you guys. You are really learning and growing in your writing ability."

One parent replies, "We are so impressed with how hard you all are working. We loved listening to your eBooks and can't wait to see what other amazing things you do!"

The young students beam as they are encouraged to continue writing and sharing their eBooks. As one student exclaims, "This is so cool! When can we write another eBook?"

Beloved children's author Mem Fox (1990) recalls receiving her first copy of *Possum Magic*: "I stroked it as if it were made of silk. This beautiful book was mine! I hugged it. I was a writer" (p. 107). An authentic publication process fosters this sense of authorship. Lucy Calkins (1994) states, "Publication . . . is the beginning, not the culmination of the writing process" (p. 266). When authors publish, they begin to see the purposeful nature of sharing their voices with an audience, and it encourages them to continue to live the writerly life. In other words, they find a sense of satisfaction when publishing that leaves many writers motivated to regularly engage in and think about writing.

For teachers like Mrs. McKinney, publication is often a goal that motivates and encourages their students to write. But finding authentic media through which to publish and share student work can be a challenge. This chapter explores how apps and online tools for digital publishing and sharing student writing beyond the classroom can foster students' confidence in their sense of themselves as writers.

Learn the Benefits of Digital Publication and Authorship

Publishing leads to the development of an identity as a writer, and developing identities as writers fosters a consciousness of and for readers. Furthermore, writing for an authentic audience is a motivating practice (Graham & Harris, 2013). Calkins (1994) suggests that this process helps writers develop insights and perceptions of themselves as readers. This insider process allows writers to develop deeper meaning and connections with the books they read.

When students write knowing they will share their work with an audience beyond the teacher, such as their peers or families, they begin to consider possibilities for publication with the reader in mind (Calkins, 1994). Students view themselves as writers when they publish their work for authentic audiences. According to Donald H. Graves (1983), "Writing is a public act, meant to be shared with many audiences" (p. 54). When students publish, they become more engaged and develop a desire to have their voices heard and valued by a wider audience than just their teacher (Dean, 2000). In so doing, students begin to realize that learning is not an isolated activity that occurs within the schoolhouse, but part of a lifelong process. Specifically, writing is a form of communication to share thoughts, opinions, and ideas for authentic purposes. People use writing every day to communicate on social media, or blog about favorite recipes, or lesson plan ideas, to name a few. To celebrate and share students' work, teachers can include student-published books in the classroom library alongside that of favorite authors, such as Kevin Henkes, Jan Brett, and Ezra Jack Keats. In this way, students can read books written by their peers as well as their favorite authors during independent reading time. Sharing writing with peers empowers authors (Lensmire, 1992).

When students share their writing with an authentic audience, they learn that their voices matter and are encouraged to continue writing (Dean, 2000). Graves (1983) explains that "children envision the appearance of a piece in print, and the teacher, parents, or friends turning the pages" (p. 54). While this is still true, digital technologies also allow students to envision readers near and far clicking the mouse and tapping the screen to read text, view images, and listen to their published writing being read aloud.

The way we read, write, and communicate is constantly shifting (ILA, 2009). New literacies augment traditional literacies to enhance learning (Bogard & McMackin, 2012) and alter the way information is created, distributed, and exchanged (Lankshear & Knobel, 2003). Using multimodal literacies has expanded the way we produce and consume texts to include multimodalities such as print, images, sound, animation, and other digital technologies (National Council of Teachers of English, 2005). Incorporating technology to foster the writing process increases engagement and motivation (Boling et al., 2008), develops a sense of community (Larson, 2009), and allows students to communicate with an authentic audience. As a result, students' writing becomes visible and valued within and beyond the four walls of the classroom. In fact, Ohler (2005/2006) states,

"Media-based stories are now everyone's to create [and] everyone's to watch and enjoy" (p. 44). The changing nature of the way we produce and share stories makes digital spaces for these endeavors more important than ever. Let's explore some ways to get started.

Access Tools That Help Students Bring Their Ideas to Life

While there are many tools, websites, and programs for publishing available, not all are useful for classroom use with elementary-age students. Table 10.1 provides information about Book Creator and Dragon Dictation, apps well suited to bringing the publication process to the classroom.

Table 10.1: Digital Tools for Digital Publication

App and URL	QR Code	Description
Book Creator www.redjumper.net/book creator		Students have a blank canvas to create and share digitally constructed text. Though the free version of the app allows the creation of only one book, it's still a good way to become familiar with the technology. The paid version of the app is ideal for a classroom.
Dragon Dictation www.nuancemobilelife.com /apps/dragon-dictation		This speech-to-text tool offers a transcription after users speak into the device. It is compatible with multiple languages. Teachers and students should note the software is not foolproof; they will need to read their transcription to ensure that it's error free.

This chapter describes Book Creator, an app that offers students a blank canvas in order to create and share digitally constructed text. The free version only allows the creation of one book but is still a good way to become familiar with the technology. However, due to this limitation, the paid version of the app is ideal for use in a classroom setting. Furthermore, the paid version offers additional stylistic options, such as a wider variety of fonts. Students can use the Book Creator app to develop a range of writing. Once authors create their books using a combination of text, images, audio, and video, they can export their finished products to share with others. To publish their work, authors can print a hard copy, create a PDF, export the digital book to eBooks, or send the file via email. The digital publication tool offers two distinct benefits: (1) the tool itself provides students with access to a variety of images, audio, and video in this interactive medium, and (2) its digital publishing options let students share their work with a large audience, one that goes beyond the classroom.

Transition to Digital Publication Using Book Creator

After downloading and opening the Book Creator app, which is available for iPad, Android, and Windows, click on New Book to begin developing a piece of writing. Our directions will follow the process for using the app on an iPad, but it is essentially the same for all versions. Select either a square, portrait, or landscape layout for the book. Next, create a book cover by adding a title and image. Students can create cover illustrations by drawing illustrations or uploading saved photos. To begin adding text, click on the plus sign (+) in the right corner. Within this window, students can modify the font, the font size, and the color, and add hyperlinks.

To add images to the book, students can click on Photos under the plus sign to insert images from the iPad camera roll. Then, they'll pinch and drag them and move them by clicking on the Arrange tab to resize the photos. Using the same plus sign symbol, students can record their voices or import music from iTunes to add sound. The pen feature provides the option for users to draw their own images. Students should click on the *i* button for options to edit any of these features.

To add a new page, click on Next or on the arrow button on the right side of the screen. Once all the pages have been created, simply click on the text to make edits. In doing so, students can make changes such as adding or deleting any text, images, drawings, and so on. Once students revise and edit their books, they should click Save. With the eBook complete, students can export their work to share it with a wider audience. From the app's home screen, students can see all of the books they created using Book Creator. To share a book listed there, simply click on the arrow and select an option for sending. The app provides many options for students to publish and share their books. Students can send them via email, import them to iTunes, post on Vimeo, add them to their collection of saved books on Book Creator, save them as PDFs, or print them as hard copies. When exporting to eBooks, the published work can be found on the digital bookshelf within the app. See "How to Create a Book With Book Creator" (wikiHow, n.d.) for more information on Book Creator and "Book Creator App Tutorial" (zakimi76, 2014) for a Book Creator Tutorial on YouTube.

Now that you understand the basics of using Book Creator, let's check in with Mrs. McKinney's kindergarten class to see how they created eBooks using the app.

Observe Book Creator in Action

To scaffold the initial learning process, students explore the Book Creator app in a teacher-led small-group setting within a literacy rotation. Mrs. McKinney works with students in groups of four to provide more individualized support, while the remaining students work in small groups in literacy centers. Mrs. McKinney shares a sample Book Creator page, then guides students using a step-by-step process to create their own page in a class eBook. She models how to insert photos, type text, change the background color, select a font, and record their reading. Mrs. McKinney gradually provides less structure and support to allow students to explore the app and create their own pages. Remaining with the small group, she observes and offers assistance when needed. Once the students demonstrate proficiency with the digital tool, Mrs. McKinney sends them off to work on their projects independently, although it is possible for students to work with peers as necessary.

The first eBooks Mrs. McKinney's students individually publish using Book Creator is titled *I Love My School Shoes!* These eBooks are modeled after Eric Litwin's (2010) well-known story *Pete the Cat: I Love My White Shoes*, which offers a predictable pattern for emergent readers and writers to mimic. The students use the camera on their iPads to take each other's pictures, capturing their friend from head-to-toe wearing his or her favorite school shoes. After inserting their photos, they change the background color of their page to match the color of their shoes. Afterwards, the students follow the predictable writing pattern to write about the color of their own shoes. Some students reference the class word wall to support their writing of *I*, *love*, *my*, and color words. Mrs. McKinney provides support for students who needed assistance with the sounds in the word *shoes*. Lastly, students record themselves reading their pages.

Once students finish writing their book using Book Creator, they export their texts to eBooks so that all students have access to their peers' writing on the class iPads. During independent writing time, students cuddle up in the reading nook with their iPad to view and listen to the texts via the app. Mrs. McKinney also saves the eBooks as videos to her device's camera roll. Then she logs onto her Vimeo account and uploads the video. Once the video is uploaded, Mrs. McKinney uses the share feature to copy embed source code that lets her display it on her class website. This allows anyone who accessed the class website, including parents and school administrators, to view and comment on the students' eBooks.

The Book Creator app allows Mrs. McKinney's kindergarten students to communicate with a wider audience through the ease of publication in multiple dimensions. Knowing that their peers, principal, as well as their parents and parents of their classmates, can view their published eBooks, students become intentional with the decisions they make about writing. For instance, they learned in their unit about writing for readers that it is important to write in complete sentences with end punctuation to indicate how the text should be read. By defining a specific audience and purpose, students create positive writing experiences that increase both engagement and stamina (Seeger & Johnson, 2014). This is critically important for 21st century learners, who must be able to collaborate and write to authentic audiences beyond the classroom (Stover & Young, 2014).

Understand Content Area Connections and Extended Applications

Students can use the Book Creator app to publish various modes of writing including narrative, informational, and opinion writing. In addition to writing stories, students can share informational writing to demonstrate their knowledge of material learned in content areas as well as opinion writing to take a stance on an issue. Using *The Important Book* by Margaret Wise Brown (1999) as a mentor text, students can easily imitate the structure to write about a range of topics studied across the curriculum. This book offers a predictable pattern that students can easily adapt for any topic. Using the sentence frame, "The important thing about . . . is . . ." students can demonstrate the main idea and important details of a passage or a concept from a given content area.

Students can also use the Book Creator app to publish opinion pieces. Examples of opinion writing include essays to emphasize the importance of healthy lifestyles as well as petition writing to prevent deforestation. Students can engage in research to provide factual information to support their claims. Additionally, students can publish eBooks to share their research about topics like biographical information of famous scientists or to teach others about mathematical concepts such as geometry.

Make Adaptations

For emergent or struggling writers as well as for ELs, using an app such as Dragon Dictation may offer a useful adaptation to create an eBook. Dragon Dictation is a speech-to-text tool that allows users to speak into their iOS device and dictate their stories. The Dragon Dictation app supports a number of languages. The app will act as a scribe and type as the student speaks. Be aware that like much speech-to-text software, the transcription will not be completely accurate. Although it is common for there to be various errors due to clarity of speech, dialect, or the lack of punctuation, the app does offer students an authentic opportunity to reread their writing to revise and edit.

By default, Dragon Dictation does not insert end punctuation, which gives writers an authentic reason to reread their work. However, writers can enable this feature in the settings menu. Simply check the box for Detect End-of-Speech. It is necessary to state the type of end punctuation needed. For instance, at the end of the sentence, the user should say *period* or *question mark* depending on the type of sentence.

Dragon Dictation allows users to easily make changes with touch editing. Simply tap on a word that needs to be corrected. Dragon Dictation will provide alternate suggestions in a drop-down list. Users can also revise a word or phrase by tapping on it to highlight then rerecording their speech or manually typing it using the keyboard. When the student is done recording and revising the printed text, he or she can tap on the arrow icon to save the text.

Book Creator is an easy-to use-digital tool that fosters greater engagement and motivation in the writing process. Its numerous features allow students to customize their books in any number of ways and share them in both print and digital formats to reach a broader audience.

In order to insert the text into the Book Creator app, students will want to use the option Send to Clipboard (figure 10.1, page 99). ELs can use the speech-to-text software to record and write in their native language as well as English. This adaptation helps struggling writers compose their ideas without becoming frustrated with spelling, letter formation, or the laborious process of writing their ideas rather than speaking them. Dragon Dictation allows emergent writers, struggling writers, as well as ELs to engage in meaningful opportunities to practice their speaking and writing skills.

I got on the diving board, carefully walked to the end of the diving board, and got ready to jump. I pushed down on the board and jumped up. My feet left the board. I felt I was flying. I splashed in the water, but I didn't go under water!

Today, I still love to jump off the diving board. I do not have to wear a life jacket. I can jump off the diving board and go all the way to the bottom of the pool!

OK

I ran to the car. I put the key in the ignition. I turned the key and started the car. We were going to my cousins house to go swimming! I was so excited because it was the day I was going to jump off the diving board!

When we got my cousins house the dog met me at the door with a big slobbery wet kiss. I quickly got my bathing suit on and ran to the pool. The pool was so big that it had a diving board and an eight foot deep end. The water was blue.

I could not wait to get in the water, but I had to wait for my mom. It felt like I was waiting for hours! Finally, she came and I was allowed to get I the water.

I played with my cousins. I watched them jump off the diving board. I thought to myself, "That looks exciting!" I just had to try. I swam to the ladder and climbed out of the pool. I marched over the diving board wearing my small, bright yellow, Sponge Bob life jacket.

Figure 10.1: Students can make this kind of story on Book Creator.

PART IV

Tools to Facilitate
Assessment and Reflection

Reading Histories

In a noisy lunchroom, the fifth-grade teachers are sitting together and discussing their lesson plans, challenges, and successes in the class-room. This collaborative reflection session is a sacred part of their daily routine and one that the teachers each benefit from. Suddenly, Ms. Hannon looks up from her sandwich and says, "I feel like I spend so much time getting to know my students as readers. It's almost as if the first few weeks of school are devoted to that very endeavor. I wish there were a way to get to know who they are as readers more efficiently."

Ms. Miller, a fellow fifth-grade teacher, smiles and says, "One way I get to know my students better in the beginning of the year is through a time line project of their reading histories."

"That sounds interesting," Ms. Hannon replies. "Tell me more!"

"The whole project takes about a week. We begin by reflecting on signif-icant memories that involve reading or listening to books. We select the most important memories, and then we organize them into a time line. You could use chart paper and markers or a website like the one we used last year."

Ms. Hannon seems excited as she replies, "That sounds perfect. Thanks!"

With that thought, the lunch period ends and Ms. Miller stands up to take her students back to the classroom. As she walks away, she thinks to herself, "I started this project so that I could learn who my students are as readers. The bonus is that my students begin to understand themselves as readers, and I think that has made a huge difference in my classroom." Ms. Miller makes a mental note to share that insight with Ms. Hannon at lunch tomorrow.

With ever-increasing attention on standardized test scores (Afflerbach, Cho, Kim, Crassas, & Doyle, 2013) as well as the focus on using leveled readers to move students up through a labeling system (Abodeeb-Gentile & Zawilinski, 2013), an inevitable result seems to be an overreliance on skill-and-drill instruction—narrowing the nuanced and complex subjects of reading and writing into individual strategies and skills to be checked off a list. Yet, incorporating reflection and metacognition into the school day is essential. Reflection is a key component of learning, and students should be encouraged to look back on their work (Afflerbach et al., 2013) as their cognitive abilities help them to determine how they will be affected by their actions as well as what their future actions might be (Bandura, 1977). Essentially, students need to know where they have been to know where they are going.

As Ms. Hannon and Ms. Miller note, it's important for teachers to know their students' histories as readers. Likewise, it's important for students to recognize themselves as readers. In this chapter, we describe digital tools to create reading histories.

Learn the Benefits of Using Digital Tools to Encourage Self-Reflection

Composing a reading history is one way to encourage self-reflection. A student's identity as a reader greatly influences his or her motivation to read and engagement in the reading process (Abodeeb-Gentile & Zawilinski, 2013; Skerrett, 2012). When creating a reading history, students recall and contemplate their past reading experiences. In doing so, this process contributes to the shaping of their reading and writing identities.

To help students explore their reading identities, teachers can scaffold the process by sharing their reading histories and modeling their process. Students can reflect on their histories as readers by thinking about which books they have read and why, as well as what literacy practices they have engaged in both in and out of school (Skerrett, 2012). This process can enable the students to consider interests (Skerrett, 2012) to equip the teacher with useful information to plan individualized instruction and book suggestions for each student.

While standards, strategies, and skills instruction are an important part of literacy learning, encouraging students to reflect on who they are as readers and writers is crucial to students' literacy development. In fact, the ways students view themselves as readers, reader identity, may have as much to do with student success as does our curriculum and standards (Abodeeb-Gentile & Zawilinksi, 2013). In the words of Abodeeb-Gentile and Zawilinski (2013), "Involving students in conversations about what and how they read is also crucial to empowering students to construct strong and positive identities as literate members of a community" (p. 41).

Access Tools for Composing Reading Histories Online

While traditional tools such as pencil and paper can certainly be used to create a reading history time line, there are several limitations to this approach. Paper has defined and constant edges. What if students' time lines are broader than the paper allows? Consider the students with large handwriting; their time lines rarely fit within the confines of a piece of paper. In order to include images, the student must hand-draw everything or paste photographs onto the paper. In this digital age, where an iPhone holds hundreds if not thousands of pictures, fewer parents are keeping traditional photographs. Rather, incorporating an online platform to create time lines allows for limitless space and uploading of photographs or images of the books students have read.

Chapter 11 focuses on using ReadWriteThink's time line tool, but there are other sites that can serve a similar purpose and are equally useful (table 11.1). With the changing technological landscape, new sites are continuously being developed. Teachers can review several sites before choosing the one that best meets the students' needs. Regardless of the site the teacher selects, the process for creating a reading history time line remains quite similar. Furthermore, the benefit for students remains the same. In crafting their digital reading histories, students gain a greater sense of their reading identities, which can inform their personal reading goals as well as the teacher's instructional goals.

Table 11.1: Digital Tools to Build Time Lines

Site and URL	QR Code	Description
Dipity www.dipity.com		Dipity allows each user to create three free time lines. Each student must sign up for an account and provide an email address. Students can make their time lines private or can work together to create a collaborative time line. The site also has a comment feature. With increased space to type and access to unmonitored content, this site may be more appropriate for older students.
ReadWriteThink Time Line www.readwritethink.org/files /resources/interactives /timeline_2		ReadWriteThink Timeline does not have as many bells and whistles as other sites, but it is an easy, free website students can use to create as many time lines as they want. No email or login information is required. One drawback is that there is not much space to type in the title bar. For example, the user will run out of space to type *Where the Red Fern Grows* in the label box.

continued →

Tiki-Toki www.tiki-toki.com		Tiki-Toki allows students to create one free time line (with infinite views) and embed images and videos. An education option allows the teacher to give fifty students access to unlimited time lines for a yearly fee. However, all students need to create their own account and provide an email address.
Timetoast www.timetoast.com		Timetoast is free for as many time lines as the user wishes to create. Students do need an email address to sign up.
VoiceThread www.voicethread.com		VoiceThread is a cloud-based application that allows students to upload, share, and discuss multimodal artifacts. Students can create free individual accounts, or teachers can set up classroom accounts for a fee. Read more about VoiceThread in chapters 12 (page 113) and 13 (page 123).
audioBoom www.audioboom.com		An easy-to-use online platform, audioBoom can be used in educational settings to record and share podcasts with peers, parents, and people from around the world.

Transition to Digitally Composing Reading Histories Using ReadWriteThink

The teacher begins by composing his or her own history to gain experience with the process and to offer students a model. After the teacher shares his or her reading memories with the class, the students then begin the process of brainstorming their own memories aloud with a partner. This provides time for an oral rehearsal as well as social interaction. After students have had a chance to discuss memories related to reading, they may use a journal or a writer's notebook to record the personal memories that they discussed with a peer. The journal can also be used as a place to continue the brainstorming process as new memories come to mind throughout the day. Students may recall favorite authors or specific text types such as magazines, books, or articles. The students can include both digital and traditional texts.

Additionally, students may also record any feelings associated with those reading materials and experiences. Students can write down memories about books that they have personally read as well as books that were read to them by parents or teachers. The memories may be positive, negative, or a combination of both. Since experiences shape students' identities as readers, the teacher can use this information to get a better sense of each student and can use that understanding in the classroom. For example, Seth may share a negative experience from when he was in third grade. As he details the panic he felt and the mistakes he made when he was asked to read aloud, his teacher, Ms. Miller, can glean some valuable information. In fact, Ms. Miller can now recognize that this might be one of the causes of Seth's lack of interest in reading as well as his low perception of himself as a reader. As a result, Ms. Miller knows to work on building Seth's confidence in reading and will most likely steer clear of asking him to read aloud in front of peers until he feels comfortable to do so.

If students struggle getting started with brainstorming, the teacher can scaffold the reflection process with some guiding questions (see "Scaffolded Reflection Question" in the appendix, page 150). We recognize that the reflection and recording process takes time and should occur over multiple sessions.

During a follow-up lesson, students can review their recorded memories and order them chronologically. This may worry some students, and you will hear resounding queries such as, "I don't remember when my mom read *Goldilocks*! Do I still need to put a date?" and "I don't remember if that was when I was six or seven! What do I do?" Remind students that they are simply trying to place their memories in chronological order to the best of their ability. This is an approximation and students should focus more on the memories instead of the specific dates that the memories occurred. For example, if Seth remembers that he read *Pete the Cat* (Litwin, 2010) to his baby sister when he was in first grade and also remembers that he read *Lincoln and Grace: Why Abraham Lincoln Grew a Beard* (Metzger, 2013) in second grade, he should place the *Pete the Cat* memory before the *Lincoln and Grace: Why Abraham Lincoln Grew a Beard* memory. Students can either rewrite the memories in chronological order, or, to save some time, the teacher can just ask that students number the memories on the left side of the paper. The teacher can remind students of the function of a time line and can show his or her own time line again, pointing out to students that earlier memories are on the left with later memories falling on the right hand side of the time line.

Once students have recorded and chronologically ordered their reading memories, they can go to the ReadWriteThink Timeline site to create their digital time lines. Since it is a lengthy URL, teachers may choose to embed the link in the class blog or post a QR code for tablets where students can easily access it. They can also google *read write think time line* to access the website. Each student will then enter his or her name and the project title into the boxes (figure 11.1, page 108).

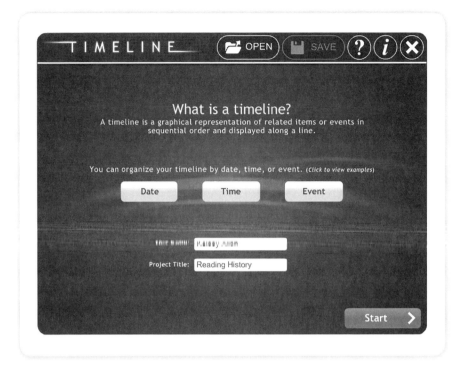

Figure 11.1: ReadWriteThink Timeline website.

See the "ABC Bookmaking Builds Vocabulary in the Content Areas" lesson by Laurie Henry, provided by ReadWriteThink.org, a website developed by the International Reading Association and the National Council of Teachers of English.

Once students fill in their name and the project title, they click on Start. Then, students can click anywhere on the time line to begin adding reading memories (figure 11.2, page 109).

Each entry allows for a label, a short description, and a full description. The label bar may not have enough space for the student to type the entire memory. In that case, the student can go down to the short description bar to finish typing. The information entered in the short description box will be seen on the time line, but will not appear on the printout. Conversely, any information typed in the full description box will be on the printout but not the digital time line.

A feature of ReadWriteThink's time line is that the student may save unfinished work. To save an unfinished time line, the student should select Save at the top of the screen and follow the prompts from ReadWriteThink. When the student is ready to return to his or her saved work, he or she should go back to the time line site and select Open at the top of the page. The student will then select Find My File and will choose his or her time line. The time line will come up and the student may continue working where he or she left off. It is important to note that the file will save to the hard drive of the computer or on the iPad, if the student is using the app. Therefore, if the student is in the lab or on a specific computer or iPad in your classroom, make sure to tell the student to get back on the same computer or iPad in order to continue the time line.

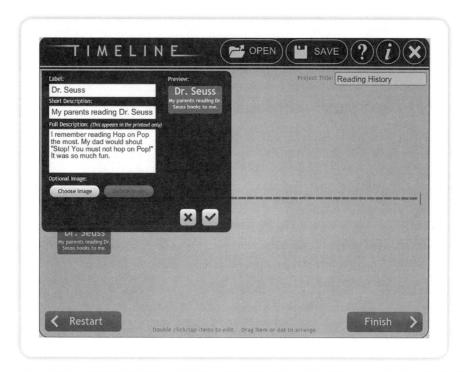

Figure 11.2: Reading history entry on the time line.

See the "ABC Bookmaking Builds Vocabulary in the Content Areas" lesson by Laurie Henry, provided by ReadWriteThink.org, a website developed by the International Reading Association and the National Council of Teachers of English.

When students have placed their reading memories in the digital time line, they can email a PDF to their teacher. If the students maintain blogs in the classroom, they might also upload the time line to their blogs. After students create their reading history time lines, they should review them and reflect about what reading has meant to them in their lives. Has reading been a mostly positive, negative, or neutral experience? Students should then write a brief reflection. If students have blogs, they may complete the reflection on their blogs and can share their reading histories and who they are as readers with their classmates and family members.

Students can also share portions of their time lines or their reflections orally with their classmates. Students can get in small groups of two to three to share and discuss their reflections. Before they begin, the teacher may want to review good listening practices such as maintaining eye contact and asking thoughtful questions. For students who seem to be struggling, the teacher can scaffold the process by providing the students with the following sentence frames.

- I hear you saying . . .
- Why do you feel that way?
- What do you think would have happened if . . . ?
- How did that make you feel?

By sharing their histories and thinking through who they are as readers, students can become more reflective and can use this experience as a springboard to set new goals for themselves as readers.

Observe ReadWriteThink Time Lines in Action

Ms. Miller's fifth-grade class creates reading histories as a way to introduce themselves as readers at the beginning of the year. In preparation for the project, Ms. Miller constructs her own reading history as a model. She feels better prepared to answer technical questions from the students after using the website to create her own. Then, Ms. Miller discusses the reflection piece and encourages her students to remember reading experiences. One student struggles to remember books that she read, so Ms. Miller suggests that she start with the books that they read together as a class. Furthermore, Ms. Miller provides her with the scaffolded questions (see the appendix, page 150) to help the student remember some of her reading experiences.

After students recall reading experiences and select some of their most powerful reading memories, Ms. Miller demonstrates how to use ReadWriteThink's time line tool and shares her own reading history as an example. After downloading the ReadWriteThink Timeline app, the students are excited and enjoy using their iPads to create their personal reading histories. In fact, Ms. Miller overhears comments such as, "I remember this book called *How to Tie Your Shoes* and it had ties and everything!" Another shares, "I remember getting my first *Clifford* book!"

The time lines allow the teacher and the students to get to know each other better as readers. For a teacher, this information can be particularly insightful, as it helps to reveal knowledge about students' experiences and preferences. For example, in the time line featured in figure 11.3 (page 111), the teacher can discern that the student does not like to read aloud in front of others and enjoys reading comics and books about President Lincoln. This information enables the teacher to make appropriate instructional decisions and helps students identify books of interest for independent reading.

After completing their time lines in Ms. Miller's classroom, students write one-paragraph reflections about their identities as readers. Before they share those reflections and the links to their reading histories time lines with one another, Ms. Miller helps the students develop class norms. She wants her students to feel safe sharing their thoughts and ideas and discusses with students that they all have different experiences. She reminds students that all those experiences were valuable. As expected, students have a range of both positive and negative reading experiences. A sense of community emerges as students share who they are as readers. Ms. Miller's classroom develops into a safe space where students feel comfortable sharing both the positives and negatives of their reading histories. Consequently, students begin recommending books more regularly and natural discussion of literature emerges as students find peers with similar reading interests. Reflecting on and sharing their reading identities also encourages students to set goals. For instance, some students decide to increase the quantity of time spent reading or the number of books read and others challenge themselves to read more complex texts. Such goals nurture greater independence and identities as lifelong readers.

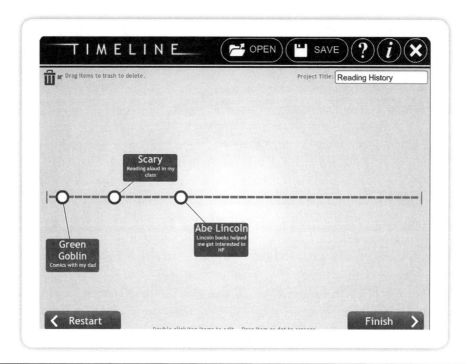

Figure 11.3: Reading history time line example.

See the "ABC Bookmaking Builds Vocabulary in the Content Areas" lesson by Laurie Henry, provided by ReadWriteThink.org, a website developed by the International Reading Association and the National Council of Teachers of English.

Understand Content Area Connections and Extended Applications

As representations of a process, time lines are well suited to use as tools for mapping sequential parts. When studying the life cycle of a plant, students can create a time line detailing the trajectory of the plant growth. The first entry on the time line might be *seed*. Students can upload a photograph of a seed and a description of that stage in the plant's growth cycle. Next, the student would describe *seedling* and the subsequent stages.

Time lines are also wonderful tools for examining history and teachers can easily integrate the digital time line into social studies. For example, students studying World War II may create a time line of important battles. Students could work in collaborative groups, discussing and deciding the most significant battles of the war. Students might also include outcomes of the war. After the group time line is completed, the teacher can upload the file or embed a screenshot of the time line on the class website.

Additionally, many informational books follow a time line format. Students can engage in retellings of the following books and study text structure by creating time lines.

- *Capital! Washington D.C. From A to Z* by Laura Krauss Melmed
- *The Boston Tea Party* by Pamela Duncan Edwards
- *Vote!* by Eileen Christelow
- *The Life and Times of the Honeybee* by Charles Micucci

- *The Honey Makers* by Gail Gibbons
- *From Seed to Sunflower* by Gerald Legg

Similarly, students can interview family members to write and share their personal family histories. To begin, the teacher might read a book such as *Seven Brave Women* by Betsy Hearne (1997) to examine how the author described the women in her family as courageous (Dorfman & Cappelli, 2009). Next, the teacher should ask students to brainstorm a list of family members whom they would like to interview. Together, generate possible interview questions such as What is your biggest accomplishment? The teacher should encourage students to choose three questions for their interviews. In a follow-up lesson, the teacher can show students how to reread their interview notes and highlight a section of the notes to write about. Students can include an anecdote or describe the person, place, or event in more detail. Students should continue to study the mentor text as an example of how to format and structure their own family history. They can share their final products using the ReadWriteThink time line, VoiceThread, or a number of other online tools. A nice feature of VoiceThread is the ability to record audio. Students could ask their family members to record an anecdote or reflection to include in their family history piece, making it multimodal and a work they will forever treasure.

Following the format and structure of creating reading histories, students can also create time lines about their writing histories. Often our *schooled identity*, or "social expectations for 'being a child in school'" consists of the stories told about us and to us based on report card data, comments in red pen on school work, as well as those told by our peers (Laidlaw, 1998, p. 129). When students construct their own literacy identities through the use of written histories, teachers are putting the onus of control back on students as they are encouraged to construct their own identities. When students revisit past work in writing, they can see what they have done, how they have grown, and it gives them ideas for what they might do next (Hansen, 2007). In fact, Jane A. Hansen (2007) writes, "As young writers develop a vision of what they can do, they see new opportunities" (p. 33).

Make Adaptations

If students are struggling to remember reading experiences, teachers may use the set of scaffolded reflection questions. Additionally, it helps to give students the opportunity to share ideas with one another before they brainstorm. This will help students to expand their thinking.

For students who struggle with the writing portion of this project, VoiceThread is a tool that the teacher can explore. With VoiceThread, instead of typing memories, students could use the built-in microphone in the iPad and post spoken memories. Additionally, students who prefer to write or hand-draw elements from their time line can take a photo and post it to VoiceThread. audioBoom is an additional option that will aid in recording spoken memories. The audio clip can be downloaded as an MP3 file and can be posted to an online time line such as one on Dipity. The audio file can also be used as a scaffold, allowing struggling writers to initially record their ideas, with the ultimate goal of writing or typing their memories into the time line.

Conferences With Readers and Writers

While it is still dark outside in the early morning hours, Ms. Goullet arrives to her classroom to prepare for the arrival of her second graders. She prepares lessons for whole-group and small-group instruction, organizes instructional materials, responds to parent emails, and follows up with the school counselor about an individual student all before the instruction day begins. Additionally, she thumbs through stacks of papers on her desk and flips through pages of the three-ring assessment notebook to see which students need review from the previous day's lessons.

As a new teacher, Ms. Goullet quickly learns how different each of her second grader's learning needs and instructional goals are. Organizing assessment data and tailoring instruction for twenty-five unique individuals overwhelms Ms. Goullet. Sometimes she uses a large three-ring binder with tabbed sections for each student as a way to organize her records. However, the binder is bulky, and it is not always handy to quickly jot down notes during on-the-spot teaching and assessment. Therefore, she often records anecdotal notes on nearby slips of paper as she observes students' misconceptions or struggles with various concepts. Once Ms. Goullet begins conferencing during readers' and writers' workshop, she finds a consistent format for note taking by including three components: (1) strengths, (2) teaching points, and (3) next steps. Ms. Goullet records this information for each student using a template she keeps on her clipboard. By far, Ms. Goullet finds this to be the most organized, effective, and efficient note-taking approach. However, she still finds this to be rather time consuming on top of all her other responsibilities as a second-grade teacher. That's when she hears about an app called Confer and decides to try it with her students.

Keeping track of students' individual strengths and weaknesses and next steps for multiple learning targets can be a daunting task for any teacher. Whether new to the profession like Ms. Goullet or seasoned veterans, teachers look for ways to improve their efficiency and efficacy in monitoring and addressing students' various needs.

Fortunately, digital tools can help manage and track critical information such as assessment data and conference notes. In this chapter, we'll examine the Confer app to record and organize digital conference notes to assist teachers with planning and implementing instruction that meets each individual learners' needs.

Learn the Benefits of Using Digital Tools for Conferencing

Formative assessment refers to ongoing informal types of evaluation that occur daily in the classroom. This ongoing assessment helps teachers determine students' strengths, areas of needed growth, and future instructional decisions. Formative assessment focuses more on process than a measure (Heritage, 2010). There are many different types of formative assessments, including student work samples, observation, and conferencing, to name a few. This chapter focuses specifically on the role of conferring as a way to work with individual students to assess their skills and habits as readers and writers while providing the opportunity for on-the-spot teaching.

Ralph Fletcher and JoAnn Portalupi (2001) remind us that each student experiences *a* writing process rather than *the* writing process. In other words, each student has his or her own unique process, with some students needing additional time for brainstorming while others will jump right into drafting. Teachers can honor each writer's process through the use of a workshop approach, where students write about self-selected topics at their own paces. Due to the diverse nature of students' abilities and processes, individually conferencing with students is essential. Conferring offers a "window into students' writing processes and insights on their decision-making capabilities" (Kissel, Miller, & Hansen, 2015, p. 9).

Conferencing is at the heart of student-teacher interactions and should occur daily (Anderson, 2000). Brian Kissel and colleagues (2013) argue that there are three essential factors to consider when conferencing: (1) students should set the agenda, (2) teachers should ask questions to help the writer make decisions without telling them what to do, and (3) conferences should be conversations between fellow writers. Fletcher and Portalupi (2001) also emphasize the importance of the teacher as a listener *and* a reader. Doing so positions the teacher as an equal and allows both the teacher and the student to have conversational roles in the conference (Anderson, 2000). This allows the teacher to ask questions and build on the student's strengths.

Conferences typically last approximately five minutes and should have a clear instructional focus (Anderson, 2000). According to Kissel et al. (2013), "Writing conferences are as diverse as the students engaged with them" (p. 7). They may help students:

- **Solve problems**—For example, What do you do when you have writer's block?
- **Follow up to see how things are going**—For example, Do you need any help?
- **Foster self-evaluation**—For example, What have you learned as a writer that you didn't know about yourself yesterday?
- **Enhance confidence**—For example, Great job bringing your character to life using the show-not-tell strategy we learned yesterday!

Using a predictable structure such as Calkins' (1994) *research, decide, teach* model, teachers can assess and offer on-the-spot teaching. It is important to note that the conference's purpose is not to fix the writing by marking it up with a red pen. Instead, Calkins (1994) argues that the goal is to help teach the writer so he or she can continue to apply the skills and practices to future works. This one-on-one, personalized instructional time is a vital aspect of any writing workshop. Using this type of approach, students will learn how to interact with their own writing and take more ownership over it, and will become more independent writers. Most importantly, teachers should show students that they care about them in conferences (Anderson, 2000).

When conferencing with students, it is paramount that teachers record notes immediately. Information can easily be blurred for a class full of students after a long day of teaching. These data can be used to plan instruction, create small groups, and provide appropriate feedback (Boyd-Batstone, 2004). Armed with a record of conference data, teachers can support differentiated instruction through identification of individual learning needs (Bates, 2013). Today's technological world makes documenting conference notes easier. Using mobile devices to create digital records of "students' in-the-moment learning" provides teachers with more time for reflection (Bates, 2013, p. 29). Access to the student data housed on a portable device also makes it easier for teachers to plan from home (Bates, 2013). Let's examine a few digital tools to make differentiation, note taking, and planning easier.

Access Tools to Convene Digital Conferences and to Manage Individual Instructional Needs

With increased access to digital tools such as the Confer note-taking app, collecting and organizing data and instructional recommendations are much easier for teachers. (Note that ongoing development and email support of Confer has ceased, with the developer devoting its resources to a new app, Snapfolio.) Rather than fumbling through stacks of paper or hauling around a huge binder with tabbed sections for each student or a manila folder with taped index cards that continually fall out, teachers can use apps such as Confer to efficiently organize conference notes. See table 12.1 (page 116) for a list of tools for conferencing with readers and writers.

Table 12.1: Digital Tools for Conferencing With Readers and Writers

Tool and URL	QR Code	Description
Confer app www.conferapp.com		This app, which is no longer under active development, enables teachers to take notes about students' work, organize students with similar needs into groups, and analyze trends over time.
Voki www.voki.com		Voki is a text-to-speech software program that allows users to create an avatar that reads aloud text students write or upload. The free version allows up to a sixty second audio recording; paid versions for classroom use allow multiple users to create and share avatars and record lengthier texts.
VoiceThread http://voicethread.com		VoiceThread is a cloud-based application that allows users to upload, share, and discuss multimodal artifacts. Free individual accounts can be created, or classroom accounts can be set up for a fee. Read more about VoiceThread in chapters 11 (page 112) and 13 (page 123).
Literator www.literatorapp.com		This free app provides teachers a tool that lets them intuitively track student progress, set goals, and share information with parents or colleagues.
Snapfolio www.snapfolioapp.com		Aligned with Common Core State Standards, this app allows teachers to take snapshots of student work and quickly assess using a scale of 1–4 in whole-group settings. The app can also record conference notes from independent and guided practice. Sort information easily to analyze instructional needs.

This tool provides an easy-to-use format to note students' strengths, teaching points, and next steps. A free version of the app (Confer Lite) is available, but we recommend the paid version (Confer) available for iPhone, iPad, and Android devices. The full version of the app allows teachers to import class lists to take notes on each student for all subject areas, including reading, writing, and even mathematics. Teachers have the option to take notes for individual students using the provided template (*tag*, *strength*, *teaching point*, and *next step*) or open-ended notes without the template. With data entered into the app using the template, teachers can view the students' information by name, date, reading level, tag, strength, teaching point, or next step.

There are multiple benefits to using this app for collecting and organizing student data. First, the app shows the teacher which students he or she has and has not conferred with recently. Regular conferences are essential in monitoring progress and providing needed individualized support to foster growth. Second, this app makes it easy to notice trends based on like needs to design appropriate instruction. Third, students can be grouped based on common next steps to foster collaboration and guided support in small-group instructional settings. This approach is more efficient than traditional note taking where the teacher records the same information over and over again for each student in the small group. Instead, the Confer app gives the user an option to select students from a small group to create a new note. By creating small groups using the Confer app, the teacher can easily access information including students' reading levels, stage in the writing process, and what the next instructional steps should be. Finally, teachers can share information easily with the Confer app. For instance, data in Confer can be emailed or uploaded to a Google account to easily create a spreadsheet with the information. It is important to note, however, that teachers should use this app on a password-protected device that students do not share in order to keep the information confidential.

Transition to Digital Conferencing Using Confer

To begin using the Confer app in your own classroom, we recommend that you first implement individual conferences with or without the app to familiarize yourself with the format and structure of this type of on-the-spot individualized assessment and instruction. Conferencing can be challenging, as it requires in-the-moment decision making (Cazden, 1988) as opposed to preplanned lessons. However, these conferences are often full of important dialogue, teaching points, and goal setting that should be recorded for future instructional decisions. Therefore, we encourage you to explore a variety of note-taking options to maintain updated records of your conferences. When you are ready to begin using the Confer app to record digital conference notes, we suggest beginning with a small group rather than the entire class. Starting small will allow you to build familiarity and comfort with the digital tool and its features. Perhaps you might begin with your struggling learners who will need more consistent and regular conferences.

To get started, set up an account in Confer and create your subject areas or periods. Within each subject or class period folder, create a class list. You can upload your class list directly or import it from Dropbox or email. To manually add students, click New then tap the plus sign and add each student's name. You can also add students' proficiency levels. This can be helpful for forming guided-reading groups. Click Save after you add your students. You can add a note to each student by selecting the student and then selecting Tag, Strength, Teaching Point, or Next Step to insert information. Although the option is available to record data in each of these four subsections, it is not required. You can add as much or as little to each field within a student's note as you desire. Additionally, you can use the Quick Text feature to copy previously recorded text from an earlier note and add multiple entries within a field (such as multiple next steps). You can also add the same note for multiple students. Select students from a small group by checking the box in front of their names and then create a new note. By tapping Add Note in the upper corner of the screen, you are taken to a new page for the small group. Here, you will see the template used for individual conferences, but any information entered in this page will automatically be saved in each individual student's online file once it is saved. This is helpful especially for a small guided-reading group where the instructional focus is the same for all group members. Be sure to always save the note once you enter the data.

To determine which students have not had a recent conference, you can sort students by date with the most recent conference notes at the bottom. This will give you a quick snapshot of who you have not met with recently so no students slip through the cracks. You may also sort notes based on the content by similar tag, strength, teaching point, or next step to determine similar instructional needs. Level View will instantly list students within the same performance level, making it easier for you to create flexible guided-reading or mathematics groups. Finally, you can sort based on individual needs. For instance, using the search box, you can type "beginnings" to see who needs support with developing engaging leads in their writing. This helps to quickly create flexible groups of students for additional support in common areas. Students can be added, disbanded, or moved between groups at any time. Additionally, you can flag students for follow-up by tapping on the small flag icon. This feature might be helpful during whole-group observations, for instance. When planning for follow-up, simply click on Flag View to see which students need additional reteaching.

Teachers can tag any digital conference notes they collect using Confer. When tagging a note, assign a key word and description for the note. These tags make it easier to search and browse for common elements within and among various conference notes. For instance, a common hashtag among second-grade writers may include *#FocusOnMainIdea*. You can search the key word "focus" and any relevant notes with this hashtag will be displayed. This feature makes data management more efficient and instructional decisions and grouping easier.

Confer gives you functional and informative data at your fingertips. You can email yourself notes, upload them to Google Docs, import a list of teaching points as a plain text file, or create printable reports. You can easily share these data with other teachers, administrators, and parents. The abilities to quickly access and share data are helpful if you share students with other colleagues throughout the day. Furthermore, if a student transfers schools, you can easily send the data to the new teacher using email, Dropbox, or a spreadsheet.

For more information about getting started with writing workshop, see Fletcher and Portalupi's (2001) *Writing Workshop: The Essential Guide*. For more information about conferencing during writing workshop, see Carl Anderson's (2000, 2005) books including *How's It Going?: A Practical Guide to Conferring With Student Writers* and *Assessing Writers*.

Observe Confer in Action

Cooper, a second grader, reads on grade level and enjoys reading and writing. His teacher, Ms. Goullet, conducts a variety of minilessons to address patterns of needed growth among her students. For instance, when she notices that many of her students' writing samples and assignments lack organization, she models and discusses how a popular author, Tomie dePaola, organizes his writing to make it flow in a sequenced manner for his readers. When reading dePaola's (1979) book, *Oliver Button Is a Sissy*, Cooper and his class point out numerous transition words such as *then*, *so*, and *finally* that dePaola uses to indicate sequence and organization. The class records these words for future reference.

Like many of his peers, Cooper can enhance his writing with development in organization and details. This is evident in his *free write* activity. In this writing sample, the students free write about any topic using any genre. While some students use this time to do journal-style writing, others reflect on previous learning or write stories. Cooper writes a story about his weekend (see figure 12.1).

Figure 12.1: Cooper's writing sample.

In her conference with Cooper, Ms. Goullet asks Cooper what his goals are for the day. He replies that he is writing about last weekend. Ms. Goullet nods enthusiastically and asks Cooper to read his story. After he reads, Ms. Goullet tells Cooper, "I like the way you write with such details Cooper. You tell us a lot about your weekend. What do you want the reader to mostly know about? In other words, what is the heart of your story?"

Cooper thinks for a moment and replies, "Well, I had fun with my friend, but I guess the best part is getting my new dog, Sparta."

"So the highlight of your weekend was spending time with your dog. This is the heart of your story," Ms. Goullet reflects back to Cooper. "Sometimes I use different revision techniques to make my writing better. One strategy I like is to highlight the heart of the story and develop a new piece just around that idea. You could reread your writing and then draw a box around the part of the story you want to develop," she continues.

"I think it should start at the part about Saturday since that is when I say we got our dog," Cooper muses.

"OK, can you show me that part?" Ms. Goullet inquires. Cooper points to the section and draws a box around it (see figure 12.1, page 119).

"Great job, Cooper! Now that you've highlighted this section, what do you think you'll do next?" Ms. Goullet prods.

Cooper says, "I'm going to keep writing from this part so my story is all about getting my new dog, Sparta."

"Great! You may even want to consider cutting and pasting this part on a new page to start writing from that part in your story. I look forward to reading your new story about Sparta!" Ms. Goullet replies.

In her conference with Cooper, Ms. Goullet positions herself as a fellow writer and helps Cooper make decisions about his writing. By rereading his piece, Cooper reexamines his purpose and considers the heart of his story, or what he really wants his readers to know more about. According to Fletcher and Portalupi (2001), "Rereading is the glue that connects the stages of writing" (p. 67). With this revelation, Cooper is fueled and ready for his next step. He will begin drafting his new piece of writing, this time staying more narrowly focused on the single event of getting his dog, Sparta.

During the conference, Ms. Goullet records notes using the Confer app (figure 12.2, page 121). She notes his strengths (S) including use of good details about his weekend as well as the use of various transition words from the bubble map they created as a class during the previous minilesson. Recording the teaching point (TP) to focus on the key aspect or heart of the story is helpful for the teacher for follow-up purposes. In this way, Cooper's teacher can remember what the specific focus of instruction is for his next conference. At this time, she can hold him accountable by asking him how he implemented the strategy of finding the heart of his story. Finally, Cooper's teacher records his next steps (NS) to develop his story focused on getting his dog with details and consider starting on a new page. She tags the note "Write into the day." This tag will be helpful when she wants to examine Cooper's and his peers' unsolicited writing examples to determine what strategies they apply independently. As a result of the conference conversation and Ms. Goullet's ability to efficiently record notes, Cooper has a clear purpose for his next steps as a writer. Using the Confer app, his teacher will be able to easily follow up with a simple tap of her finger to retrieve useful data from previous conferences to inform future instruction. The Confer app helps Ms. Goullet better individualize instruction and meet all learners' needs.

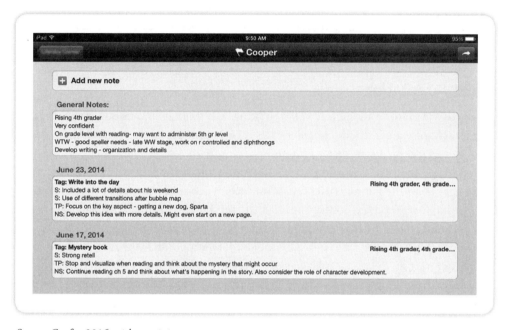

Source: Confer, 2016, with permission.

Figure 12.2: Cooper's Confer app conference notes.

Understand Content Area Connections and Extended Applications

The Confer app can be used to set up classes and record notes in any subject area. This digital tool is particularly useful when conferencing during reading and writing workshop, as Ms. Goullet demonstrates in her conference with Cooper. It also is helpful when meeting with small groups during guided reading, mathematics, and word study. In this section, we share how the app can be used to collect and organize student data during word study. Students' invented word spellings are assessed and used as a guide for differentiated instruction in phonics, spelling, and vocabulary.

During word study, students engage in hands-on learning to manipulate words in order to find generalizations and patterns that can be applied to other words and word families. Knowing that students in any given classroom represent diverse ability levels, it is important for the teacher to assess students and provide word study instruction and activities within their appropriate developmental level. Rather than a one-size-fits-all approach, teachers can group students based on their level of word knowledge. As a result, it is essential that teachers track the instruction and progress of each student. The Confer app can be used to harness information in digital forms, making data collection more efficient and effective. Teachers can use the Confer app template during word study to record students' strengths, teaching points, and next steps. For instance, in a typical third-grade classroom, some students may be studying short and long vowel patterns (*hop* and *hope*) while others are exploring less common vowels and dipthongs (*oi, ou, au*) or common homophones (*bear* and *bare*). It is important that the teacher note how students are progressing within this stage of spelling and developing word knowledge of the skills.

Make Adaptations

Text-to-speech software such as Voki can be used to facilitate independent conferences. Using such software to conduct conferences is an important step before conferring with a teacher, as it provides students with an opportunity to interact with their writing in a self-regulated manner. According to Chase Young and Katie Stover (2013/2014), "To build agency in the young writers, it is important for students to attempt their own revisions and edits before conferring with the teacher" (p. 270). By privately revising and editing before a teacher conference using an avatar such as Voki, students' text is transformed into speech and is read by the selected avatar. The verbatim read-aloud of the written text by the avatar makes it easier for students to self-evaluate. This provides a scaffold leading to self-discovery of necessary revisions and edits before conferring with the teacher. "Telling a student that his or her story is difficult to understand is less effective than allowing the student to discover it for himself or herself" (Young & Stover, 2013/2014, p. 271).

Students can also use the online tool and app VoiceThread to post their writing for online conferences with peers or parents. VoiceThread offers a variety of options and filters to limit or expand the audience. Additionally, students can share their writing in multiple modalities including uploading a photo or screenshot of their work or adding audio of themselves reading the piece aloud. This is often helpful, as it offers the first level of revision where students can revisit their work simply by reading it aloud to themselves. They can play back the recording and listen to themselves read to self-evaluate for focus, organization, details, or even word choice. Once the writing is shared with an extended audience, students can request specific feedback using the comment feature (Stover & Young, 2014). For instance, a writer may leave a comment to ask the reader to provide feedback on clarity. This step can be used before and after a conference with the teacher. By obtaining authentic feedback in this manner, the student can make revisions to do his or her best work before meeting with the teacher for a one-on-one conference. Additionally, it also works nicely for the student to implement the next steps and feedback offered by the teacher during the one-on-one conference and then request feedback from the broader audience to evaluate the revisions' effectiveness.

Digital Portfolios

It is 9 a.m. on a hot and humid South Carolina morning when nine-year-old James bounds through the doors of the Furman University library with his tablet tucked under his arm, heading straight for the table where he and his tutor, Mrs. McKinney, meet daily as part of the Literacy Corner summer reading clinic. This is quite a shift from James's usual withdrawn and shy demeanor. Previously, he clung to his mom, rarely made eye contact with others, and reluctantly participated in instructional activities.

Assessment data reveal James's low academic performance and self-perception as a reader and writer. In fact, his results from the Writing Attitude Survey (Kear, Coffman, McKenna, & Ambrosio, 2000) indicate that James is in the second percentile compared to his peers in terms of his attitude toward writing. James lacks independence and motivation as a writer. He has difficulty beginning writing and engaging in writing over multiple extended periods of time.

In addition, homework is typically a challenge to complete, and James's parents and teachers experience difficulty with encouraging him to open up and articulate his thinking and cognitive processing. When asked if he has any questions, James often looks down and shrugs. Aware of James's shy demeanor and his low self-perception as a writer, Mrs. McKinney considers alternative instructional activities that will allow him to demonstrate his understanding beyond written tests or verbal communication.

Mrs. McKinney introduced James to the Seesaw app, an online portfolio where James self-selects and uploads artifacts as evidence of his learning. Since James enjoys using technology, Mrs. McKinney believed this could increase his motivation and engagement, and she was right. She encourages James to use the Seesaw app to upload examples of his work from their tutoring sessions as a way to foster reflection and share his progress with his parents. Additionally, Mrs. McKinney is able to use the app to provide James with feedback and feedforward, further enhancing his learning opportunities.

Douglas Fisher and Nancy Frey (2009) use the term *feedforward* to refer to the use of assessment data to plan future instruction. Whereas feedback tends to be at the individual level, feedforward describes the process of making instructional decisions. This shift from measurement to modifying instruction propels learning forward. Dynamic formative assessment provides teachers and students with useful feedback to support continuous growth (ILA, 2013). Feedback is an important component of formative assessment, and it should be relevant, constructive, specific, and helpful to students (Roskos & Neuman, 2012).

But sometimes, students like James struggle to demonstrate what they know and understand. Like Mrs. McKinney, teachers often must think outside the scope of traditional assessments to provide relevant, constructive, specific, and helpful feedback to students who may struggle with self-expression. In this chapter, we'll examine how teachers can use students' digital portfolios to assess learning.

Learn the Benefits of Using Digital Tools for Feedback and Feedforward

Perhaps one of the most obvious ways to foster learning from constructive feedback from formative assessments is to make the assessment authentic. According to Hansel Burley and Margaret Price (2003), authentic assessment "focuses on analysis, integration, creativity, and written and oral expression" (p. 193). Giving students the opportunity to be actively involved in the learning and assessment process makes it more meaningful.

One way to authentically engage students in the assessment process is through digital portfolios. Digital portfolios act as a container for multimodal work samples including text, audio, visual, and hypertext to demonstrate a range of purposes and processes (Abrami & Barrett, 2005). The flexibility in terms of format as well as function allows students to individualize their online portfolios to represent their own learning and development. Students can share work in progress as well as learning over time. The online nature of the portfolios makes it easy for students and teachers to return to previous work without digging through stacks of papers.

An additional benefit of portfolios is that they allow students to become active participants in their learning through reflection of their learning processes and challenges along the way. Revisiting an online record of artifacts can help students think critically about their work, set learning goals, and share their work with an extended network. Furthermore, the online nature of digital portfolios makes it easier to connect with an authentic audience to share work and receive feedback (Merchant, 2005). This feedback can come from the teacher, peers, and parents. For instance, Brian Kissel, S. Michael Putman, and Katie Stover (2013) examine how fourth graders use a wiki as a digital portfolio to share and communicate about their writing with their peers.

Finally, digital portfolios strengthen the connection between school and home by making it easier to communicate with parents regularly about their student's progress

(Merkley, Schmidt, Dirksen, & Fuhler, 2006). Let's explore some digital tools well suited for creating student-driven online portfolios in elementary classrooms.

Access Tools as Media for Creating and Sharing Students' Online Portfolios

Teachers can easily use several online applications for student-driven digital portfolios that collect and showcase student work (see table 13.1). SeeSaw, Evernote, VoiceThread, Weebly, and KidBlog are digital tools that can be used as online portfolios for student work. Although this chapter focuses on the use of SeeSaw, these other tools can be used in a similar fashion by uploading content through text, images, and audio and video files. Content can be shared with an authentic audience, including parents and peers. Collecting students' work in an online space also makes it easier for the teacher to access student work for assessment and instructional purposes at any time from anywhere.

Popular website and app Seesaw (http://web.seesaw.me) provides a digital learning journal appropriate for students as young as five years old. Students can upload images as well as audio and video files to this safe and secure website or app. Online portfolio entries can include examples of student work, such as a photo of mathematics problems, audio to reflect on their writing processes, or a video of a performance task. Using Seesaw, students can organize their work in one place, making it easily accessible for the teacher and parents. Since the website is a secure private portfolio, parents must sign up for a free account to gain access to their child's work. Parents receive instant updates alerting them each time the teacher approves their child's recent upload in their SeeSaw portfolio. Similar to Facebook, Seesaw allows parents to like and leave comments on their student's posts. This regular communication makes a stronger school–home partnership by keeping the parents abreast of students' progress and involving them in providing feedback.

Table 13.1: Digital Tools for Digital Portfolios

Tool and URL	QR Code	Description
Seesaw website and app http://web.seesaw.me		Seesaw is an easy-to-use website to archive student work and share that work with a wide audience. A special section of teacher resources on the website provides tutorials and activity ideas for grades K–12. Seesaw is also available as an iOS app.
Evernote https://evernote.com		Evernote is an online workspace to collect, discuss, and present information.

continued →

VoiceThread http://voicethread.com		VoiceThread is a cloud-based application that students and teachers can use to upload, share, and discuss multimodal artifacts. Teachers and students can create free individual accounts, or teachers can set up a classroom account for a fee. Read more about VoiceThread's applications in chapters 11 (page 112) and 12 (page 122).
Weebly www.weebly.com		Weebly is a drag-and-drop website where users can create multimodal e-portfolios.
Kidblog http://kidblog.org		Kidblog is a safe classroom-blogging website where students can share their writing with an authentic audience other than the teacher. Read more about Kidblog's uses in the classroom in chapter 3 (page XX).

Transition to Implementing Digital Portfolios Using Seesaw

When implementing digital portfolios in your classroom, you may want to begin by considering your vision, purpose, audience, and logistics for the digital portfolios. Regardless of the platform you select for your students' digital portfolios (see table 13.1 for suggestions), you will need to begin by creating an account and setting up a class. With the online tool ready, discuss the idea of portfolios as a container of work with your students. When you introduce the selected online tool to your students, it is helpful to discuss the purpose and establish some guidelines. You might consider recording the guidelines on chart paper as a reference for students. For example, you may collectively decide with your class that students should only upload work at certain times, select their own name from the class list to ensure they post to their own accounts, and ask permission before viewing others' accounts.

With clear guidelines in place, begin by modeling how to add an item to the online portfolio. Print the sign-in document from Seesaw and show students how to use the QR code to open the app.

Next, demonstrate how to take a photo of a work sample (perhaps an example of your own writing to model for students) and then use the voice recorder to explain or reflect on the piece. Model for students the kinds of questions they may consider when reflecting on their work. For instance, students may reflect on their strengths and areas for growth based on evidence in the work sample. This is helpful when comparing entries to previously saved portfolio items, highlighting growth over time.

Students may also examine the process they experienced when developing the piece. For example, a student may note that when he published his narrative story, it was initially difficult to find a topic, but once he did he was able to easily write a draft. Upon rereading his writing, he realized that he needed to revise by using more precise language and omitting redundancy.

Additionally, students can consider areas for continued growth and next steps for goal setting. Throughout this process, students can be held more accountable and will develop more ownership in their learning process.

When students are ready to post their work and any reflection, show them how to find the correct name from the class list to ensure they posted in the correct student portfolio. You will need to approve all submissions before they are posted online.

Observe Seesaw in Action

Eli and James, both nine-year-old students enrolled in the Literacy Corner summer reading program at Furman University, are paired with Mrs. McKinney, a kindergarten teacher and graduate student pursuing a master's degree in literacy education. Mrs. McKinney tutors Eli and James in a one-on-one setting. Since both boys are struggling readers and writers, it is essential that Mrs. McKinney documents their progress and clearly communicates with both sets of parents. She uses Seesaw to help students create a digital portfolio of their work during the program.

Mrs. McKinney begins by creating a class on Seesaw, and parents are sent an invitation to join. Each student has his own digital portfolio and accesses it during each tutoring session to upload work samples and reflect on his progress. Students evaluate their progress by examining strengths and areas for continued practice. This leads to goal setting and student-facilitated instructional agendas.

Although both students are the same age, Eli and James have different interests, personalities, learning styles, and academic needs. James is typically shy and reserved. He needs support with writing skills and increasing his perception as a writer. To help James become an "initiator of writing" (Anderson, 2005, p. 21), Mrs. McKinney encourages him to write for various purposes, use a range of genres, and write for real audiences. Additionally, she taps into James's interests and values his ideas and experiences by allowing him to self-select writing topics. Being an avid fisherman, James chooses to write about fishing. He cannot wait to get started on his writing about his fishing trip over the weekend. Using the Book Creator app, James writes an opinion piece and informational pieces such as lists of different kinds of fish and tools for bait and fishing (figures 13.1 and 13.2, pages 128–129). He enthusiastically adds personal photos and then uploads his pages to the Seesaw app to share with his parents.

Figure 13.1: James's opinion writing.

After working with Mrs. McKinney in the Literacy Corner, James's score on the post-attitudinal assessment indicates that he is now in the 44th percentile, a significant increase from only four weeks earlier. As a result of the individualized approach and using technology, Mrs. McKinney helps James to increase his confidence and interest in writing. She uses online tools including the Book Creator app to nurture James's engagement in his writing process and Seesaw to share his work with an authentic audience. According to Mrs. McKinney, "Technology was definitely the gateway that changed James's view of writing!"

While James is initially quiet and reserved, Eli opens right up and interacts with Mrs. McKinney immediately. There is some overlap in the two students' instructional needs, but assessments reveal that Eli benefits most from developing as a fluent reader. The Seesaw app allows Mrs. McKinney to provide individualized feedback and encourage each unique learner's self-reflection. She knows the value of repeated reading in developing fluency, so she encourages Eli to read his text multiple times and evaluate his fluency by noting accuracy, expression, and phrasing. In order to facilitate this process, Eli uses the Seesaw app to record himself reading and self-evaluate his work. After listening to his first recorded reading, Eli notes that his reading is good since he read all the words

Source: Seesaw, 2016, with permission.

Figure 13.2: James's informational writing.

correctly, but it lacks expression. Therefore, he reads it a second time and records it on Seesaw. Eli remarks that the second reading is good because he makes his voice sound like the people are talking.

Mrs. McKinney notices an increase in parent involvement since using Seesaw with her students. Parents note the similarities between Seesaw and Facebook, where they can like and comment on their student's work frequently. Leaving a simple comment such as, "Awesome! Great job James," is positive reinforcement for James and motivates him to continue developing his writing. This type of communication and support from home is widely believed to be a vital component to student success (Paratore, 2011). Ongoing feedback related to the learning goals validates student progress while offering suggestions to improve learning. Feedforward can be both teacher and student driven. When considering how the data influence instructional decisions, the student can reflect on his or her own next steps through goal setting. Seesaw makes this interaction instant and interactive and provides an effective way to share work samples on a daily or weekly basis, rather than waiting to share and discuss at the end of the quarter during parent conferences.

Toward the end of the summer reading program, Mrs. McKinney encourages the students to use the note-taking feature to revisit and reflect on previous work. Mrs. McKinney uses the following sentence frames for reflection to scaffold this process.

- As a reader, I have learned . . .
- To continue to grow as a reader, I will . . .
- As a writer, I have learned . . .
- To continue to grow as a writer, I will . . .

Students use these sentence frames as they add text and voice recordings to journal items to reflect, explain, and set goals.

Seesaw provides several options to help students demonstrate their learning and post their reflections. For example, James is not confident recording his voice, so he prefers to use photos and the written comment feature to reflect. James types responses to the sentence starters to reflect on his progress as a reader and a writer in general. Considering that James is reluctant to do any writing in school, or at the beginning of the summer reading program, Mrs. McKinney is thrilled when he comments that his goal is "To continue to grow as a writer, I will keep writing" (see figure 13.3). This indicates that James understands the importance of writing to foster growth and may demonstrate his future propensity to initiate independent writing.

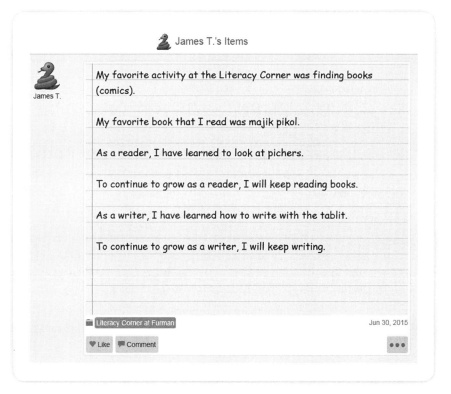

Source: Seesaw, 2016, with permission.

Figure 13.3: James's reflection.

Seesaw works well to accommodate each student's learning styles and needs. The technology Mrs. McKinney incorporates to share feedback and the students' self-evaluation result in both Eli and James increasing their motivation as readers and writers. By the end of the program, they are well on their way to developing the necessary skills for becoming independent readers and writers.

Understand Content Area Connections and Extended Applications

Teachers can use digital portfolios across all subject areas. With increasing emphasis on problem-solving skills, Seesaw is a useful tool for students to practice multistep word problems in mathematics. Students can begin by taking a photo of their mathematics work and uploading it to Seesaw. Next, the students record themselves as they restate the problem in their own words and think aloud to consider appropriate problem-solving strategies. This allows students to document how they use a variety of strategies to solve a problem. It is helpful to model this process for all students. For instance, provide students with sentence frames such as "The problem is asking me to . . ." and "First, I need to . . ." to help them understand the steps of the process.

Some students may require more scaffolding throughout the process. For example, Kaitlyn, a third grader, describes multiple ways to solve a multiplication problem using repeated addition, a base ten method, and a drawing. When Kaitlyn first records her process for problem solving, she simply states that she knows the answer is 24 because 8×3 equals 24. To prompt Kaitlyn to dig deeper and explain her problem-solving process, her teacher encourages her to go back to her Seesaw entry and use the sentence frames to describe her problem-solving process. After listening to and reflecting on her feedback, Kaitlyn returns to Seesaw to provide a richer description of her thinking.

In her second recording on the Seesaw work sample, Kaitlyn explains: "The problem is asking me to think about how many cookies Mr. Jones needs to make so there's enough for the birthday party. First, I need to see how many people will be at the party. Then, I need to think about how many cookies each person can have. I can draw a picture to help me or I can add 3 cookies 8 times since there are 8 people going to the party."

Using Seesaw to record her problem-solving process helps the teacher determine Kaitlyn's level of understanding of the mathematical process beyond simple memorization of facts. Visit Seesaw's Activity Ideas K–2 (http://goo.gl/0Btu9Y) for more ideas. (Visit **go.SolutionTree.com/technology** to access live links to the websites mentioned in this book.)

Make Adaptations

In flipped classrooms, teachers and students can use Seesaw to create video and audio recordings for preteaching and reviewing content using a blended model. Teachers give students the link to the online tutorial to watch before class time, typically outside of the classroom.

Teachers can also use this approach with students who need reinforcement and review of the material. Students who are absent from school due to illness, for instance, can watch the videos and leave comments or questions for their peers or the teacher to respond. This ongoing dialogue engages students in the learning process and provides them with authentic opportunities to develop communication and collaboration skills. Furthermore, when students record their explanations on Seesaw, they deepen their own understanding.

Through this type of blended learning, students are no longer limited to learning in isolation within the classroom's boundaries. Instead, digital learning tools provide students with additional opportunities to learn the material in various ways beyond the traditional sit-and-get lecture method in the classroom. Finally, Seesaw enhances communication with parents as they develop a better understanding of expectations after viewing the online lectures and activities themselves, leaving them better equipped to provide additional support at home.

Digital Formative Assessment of Reading Comprehension

Like many classroom teachers, Ms. Hale assigns quizzes and tests to measure her students' literacy performance. Each Friday, her students answer multiple-choice comprehension questions about the story they read that week. Additionally, all students in the school district complete benchmark tests to measure comprehension on grade-level passages each quarter. Some students read closely, noticing and recording their thinking in the margins, while others appear to read rather quickly and simply circle one of the four possible answer choices. Students also take online comprehension tests to determine their independent reading level and measure growth.

However, the aforementioned multiple-choice comprehension assessments do not provide Ms. Hale with insight into all students' thinking. Students can easily circle an answer choice without putting much thought into it or without truly understanding the material they read. Therefore, Ms. Hale decides that she needs to find a way to assess students' thinking by accessing their active metacognitive process as readers. She teaches students to record their thinking about the text being read by stopping and jotting their connections, questions, predictions, and statements on sticky notes before, during, and after reading. Later she asks students to discuss their sticky notes during individual conferences. In real time, Ms. Hale can determine each student's level of cognition. Additionally, setting aside time for individual conferences allows Ms. Hale to ask students to clarify or elaborate on their thinking in a conversational manner. All these measurements combine to give Ms. Hale a better understanding of each student's reading ability.

Often, teachers like Ms. Hale use traditional assessments such as exams, end-of-grade standardized tests, and quizzes in their classrooms. As Stephanie Harvey and

Anne Goudvis (2007) attest, assessment is the "heart of teaching and learning" (p. 7). Assessment and instruction are inextricably linked as one constantly informs the other. With the goal of teaching to enhance learning and deepen understanding, it is vital that educators know the degree to which students comprehend the material and adjust instruction accordingly.

In this chapter, we examine digital tools that support formative assessments of students' reading comprehension.

Learn the Benefits of Using Digital Tools to Assess Comprehension and Understanding

Depending on the stakeholder involved, a different ethos prevails regarding the function and value of assessments. Summative assessments are typically given at the end of a unit or grade (McNair, Bhargava, Adams, Edgerton, & Kypros, 2003; Roskos & Neuman, 2012) and are generally used for accountability and reporting (McNair et al., 2003). Unfortunately, due to the lack of time in most teachers' days, summative assessments do not typically allow teachers to go back and reteach material (Roskos & Neuman, 2012). Policymakers tend to think of assessment as a way to hold educators accountable, while teachers are more likely to consider assessment as a method to determine what a student can do now, can't quite do yet, and should be able to do soon (Casbergue, 2011).

In contrast, formative assessments are continuous and informative and provide data to help teachers reflect on instructional decisions quickly (McNair et al., 2003; Roskos & Neuman, 2012). According to the International Literacy Association's (2009) position statement, formative assessment should be purposeful, collaborative, and dynamic to support ongoing development. Formative assessment helps inform instruction (Fiene & McMahon, 2007) and more closely mirrors authentic literacy practices.

Comprehension is one such complex process that cannot be easily measured in isolation (Stover & Yearta, 2015). Therefore, gathering data from multiple sources can help teachers gain insight into student thinking to help tailor needed instruction. Reader response is one way readers can demonstrate their understanding, by interacting with text in meaningful ways and making those interactions visible to their teacher. Traditionally, this may have taken the form of notes in the margin, one-on-one conversations, reader-response journals, or thoughts recorded on sticky notes.

With the prominence of technology in classrooms, reader response can be moved to a digital platform to allow students to share their thinking regularly and with ease. Not only do digital tools make it easier for students to share their thoughts, these tools also allow teachers to access student thinking at any time from any place through online posts related to the students' reading. Let's look at some digital tools and platforms that support these aims.

Access Easy-to-Use Tools for Assessing Comprehension

Many digital platforms and spaces, such as Padlet and Lino, enable students to curate, compile, and share information (table 14.1). In this chapter, we'll focus on Lino, an online corkboard for students to add their *stop-and-jots*, or thoughts about the text they are reading.

Table 14.1: Digital Tools to Assess Comprehension

Tool and URL	QR Code	Description
Lino website and app http://en.linoit.com		Lino is a free website and app that allows students and teachers to compile and post sticky notes, photos, videos from YouTube and Vimeo, and other file types to an online canvas.
Padlet https://padlet.com		Padlet is an online corkboard where users can easily add content with a simple click of a mouse or double tap of a tablet. Sharable content includes text, hyperlinks, YouTube videos, and photos.

Lino is a website and app for iPhones, iPads, and Androids that serves as a corkboard where users can post sticky notes, photos, and videos from YouTube and Vimeo to multiple canvases. In fact, you can post and share any kind of file. Students can customize digital sticky notes with different colors, fonts, and sizes. They can tag notes by typing in the key words in the tag line, making it easier to search and group similar notes. Users can create multiple boards for a number of purposes.

For instance, Lino can be used as a place for students to communicate with their peers by posting digital sticky notes about a shared text being read in a book club. Another option is for students to post their stop-and-jots during independent reading in order to later discuss with the teacher during a conference. Furthermore, Lino can be used as a way to preassess students' knowledge of a particular topic. The teacher can introduce the subject and ask students to record what they know and what they wonder about the given topic.

Depending on the purpose of the Lino board, access can be private or shared with others for collaboration. When creating a new canvas, simply click on one of the following options: private use, show sticky notes to everyone, or allow everyone to post sticky notes. By updating this setting, the teacher can easily change the privacy of, and access to, Lino posts accordingly.

Once a Lino canvas is created, users can easily post sticky notes by clicking on the selected color sticky note, typing in the box, and saving the note. Sticky notes can be augmented with the addition of images, videos, and other attachments. To add multimedia, the student simply selects the type of file to upload and follows the on-screen instructions. Sticky notes, photos, and videos can be easily moved around the canvas in order to organize the layout by clicking or tapping and dragging. Notes can be edited, shared, copied to another canvas, or deleted. In addition, other features of Lino include posting reminders for due dates and deadlines in the calendar and finding the latest sticky notes by clicking on Highlight New. Tablet users can zoom in and out of the canvas by pinching touch screens. My Page provides an overview of individual and group canvases as well as any due dates.

Transition to Digital Stop-and-Jots Using Lino

To begin using Lino in your classroom, go to http://en.linoit.com, where you can also download the app version for iPhone, iPad, or Android. You can begin a trial canvas without even signing up. However, to take advantage of all of the features Lino offers, we recommend signing up for a free account. Create your account with a username, password, and email address, and then sign in. This will take you to the home page, or My Page. From this page, you can create and easily access a myriad of private or shared canvases. Lino also has a feature to create groups. This is helpful if you want to create

 small groups for guided reading or book clubs where students can access the shared space to contribute collaboratively. It also allows you to keep your teacher Lino boards separate from student Lino boards. You can personalize the different Lino board backgrounds with wallpaper or images of your choice. Visit www.youtube.com /watch?v=QItimc1_BgI for a short video to learn how to navigate Lino.

Observe Lino in Action

Ms. Hale introduces her fifth graders to the concept of stop-and-jots during her read-aloud of the book *Home of the Brave* by Katherine Applegate (2007). In the first week of school, Ms. Hale explains that each day she will read aloud to the class before reader's workshop. Then students will have opportunities to read self-selected books, participate in book clubs, and use technology to record reader responses and communicate with other readers. While reading chapter 1, Ms. Hale uses sticky notes to model how to record tracks of her thinking about the text, or what she calls *stop-and-jots*. She encourages the students to also record their thinking on a sticky note during the read-aloud. At the end of the chapter, Ms. Hale invites students to share their stop-and-jots with their peers.

On the next day, Ms. Hale reads chapter 2 of *Home of the Brave*. However, this time, she explains to her students that she will be posting her stop-and-jots on the computer. She displays the Lino website on the Smart Board and models the logistics of posting online sticky notes in Lino. "Just like we recorded our thinking on real sticky notes yesterday, we can instantly stop and jot down our thinking using these online sticky notes. The benefit is that everyone can see my thinking instantly," Ms. Hale explains.

Each day during the read-aloud for the next two weeks, Ms. Hale encourages her fifth graders to practice using Lino by logging into their iPads and laptops to record their thinking. Students show a range of observable comprehension skills. They analyze and compare characters and lift favorite lines from the text. Additionally, evidence from one stop-and-jot demonstrates how one student develops a worldview by considering privilege in the United States.

After familiarizing students with the concept of stop-and-jots and the processes to use Lino, Ms. Hale sets up individual Lino boards for each student to begin stop-and-jots for independent reading. Based on initial assessments, Ms. Hale helps students find books within their independent reading levels. Nardos and Olivia both select the book *Ungifted* by Gordon Korman (2012), whereas Natasha and Ian select *Bridge to Terabithia* by Katherine Paterson (1977). *Ungifted* is a higher-level text that deals with several complex social issues. *Bridge to Terabithia* is a classic novel about children who create a magical kingdom to escape bullies. Each day during independent reading, the fifth graders read at their own pace and record their thinking on their individual Lino boards. Ms. Hale uses this as a method of informal assessment to determine students' understanding of the text and ways that she might adjust instruction to address misconceptions or continue nudging them to think deeper. See figure 14.1.

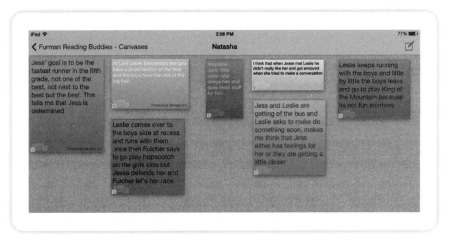

Source: Infoteria Corporation, 2016, with permission.

Figure 14.1: Natasha's Lino canvas board.

For example, after observing Natasha's stop-and-jots from September 15, Ms. Hale notices that Natasha demonstrates basic comprehension of story events and is ready to dig deeper with inferential thinking. The following day, Ms. Hale confers with Natasha to teach her how to move beyond surface-level understanding of the text.

"Hi Natasha, from looking at your sticky notes I see that you're a very observant reader, and you jot down subtle events that are happening in the story. For instance, you wrote that Jessie would play with the boys, but one by one, they left her to go play something else. I noticed that too! I think you are ready now to write about what this makes you think is really happening in the story. This is called inferring. What can you infer is the reason why the boys are leaving Jessie? Whenever you jot down another important event, I'd love to see you also add what this makes *you* think about the event. One way you can do this is by saying something like 'I think this is happening because . . . ' Give it a shot!"

Like Natasha's posts, Olivia's earliest posts on Lino indicate strong reading skills. For example, in one of her sticky notes (see figure 14.2) she lists characters as a way to keep up with them as they appear in the text. Four days later, Olivia begins commenting about the main character, Donovan, noting, "It seems to me that Donovan makes a lot of bad choices. Like escaping out the window before his detention was over." Over time, Olivia posts more sticky notes that deal with character analysis and the relationships between characters.

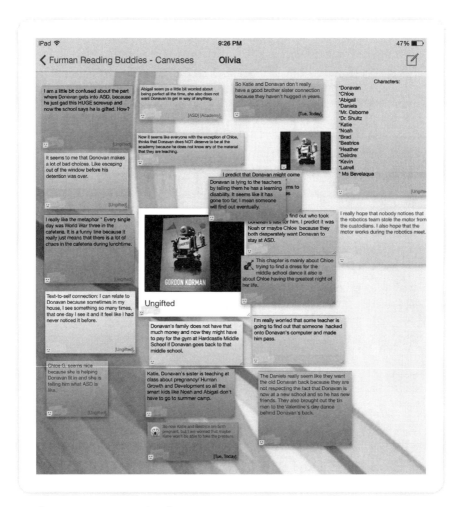

Source: Infoteria Corporation, 2016, with permission.

Figure 14.2: Olivia's Lino canvas board.

Nardos's stop-and-jots reveal evidence of her understanding of text structure, making predictions, and self-monitoring her comprehension with questioning. For example, when she comments that she likes the hypothesis sections at the onset of each chapter, Nardos's stop-and-jots indicate her awareness of the text structure. Nardos makes numerous predictions about the text, such as, "I have a feeling that something is going to go wrong with the robot. It might break!"

The act of asking questions before, during, and after reading is an effective way to engage with the text and monitor understanding. Nardos jots, "I think that Abigail almost hates Donavon, maybe as a kid he did something bad to her? I wonder why she isn't giving him a chance?" Nardos is expressive, often speaking directly to the characters in her sticky notes. (For example, she posted "Congratulations Beatrice!" when Beatrice, the family dog, had puppies.) This demonstrates that Nardos reads closely and connects with the characters on a deeper level, comprehending each character's complexities. For instance, she demonstrates understanding of Donovan's character development when she notes, "Donavon is a good kid, he just doesn't know it yet!"

In addition, Nardos effectively uses tags in her stop-and-jots. For example, she tags some with characters' names, making it easier to sort her notes based on character. This is helpful—particularly when analyzing and comparing character traits and motives.

Using students' stop-and-jots on Lino as a type of informal assessment helps Ms. Hale assess her fifth graders' reading abilities. Using these data, Ms. Hale individualizes instruction during one-on-one conferences. Her observations from the students' Lino canvases also enable her to thoughtfully design whole-group minilessons and small-group guided reading lessons to meet students' needs as readers. As a result of this intentional assessment-based instruction, Olivia learns how to jot different kinds of thinking, including story reactions and inferences. She also learns questions to ask herself during reading, such as, "How is . . . feeling?" or "How does the author use figurative language?" According to Olivia, "I am now responding to reading in a stronger way. Now I know eleven new ways to write on my sticky notes." Nardos shares, "I learned to ask myself questions and think about what a specific sentence really means! I also learned to try and figure out what the author is trying to tell or show me! I now can respond to my reading strongly and I have some pretty strong sticky notes!"

To help students self-assess and develop their comprehension, Ms. Hale develops a rubric for their stop-and-jots (see figure 14.3, page 140). By providing students with specific indicators of the ratings, both students self-assess their stop-and-jots. They then determine next steps in order to reach the goal of four stars. For example, talking about a lesson that the character learned earns three stars. When the student self-reflects and discusses her work with Ms. Hale, she determines that she needs to specifically identify how the character handles the problem, discuss any changes in that character's actions, and use textual evidence to support her statement to earn four stars. This process enables students to become more responsible for their own learning.

Stop-and-Jot Rubric

- Says what's in the book
- Names a feeling or character trait
- No text evidence
- Not detailed

- Makes a prediction
- Identifies a feeling and why
- Identifies a problem or solution
- More detail, but no text evidence

- Makes predictions, checks, and adjusts
- Talks about lesson learned
- Changes in character or patterns in book
- One piece of evidence

- Identifies how the character handles the problem
- Notices changes in characters' actions or feelings
- Develops theories (ideas) about the character
- Multiple pieces of text evidence

Your goal each and every day—

 !!!

Source: Infoteria Corporation, 2016, with permission.

Figure 14.3: Stop-and-jot rubric.

Understand Content Area Connections and Extended Applications

Encouraging students to engage in conversations about the world around them can sometimes be difficult. To engage in current events, students can read and report on an article from print and online news sources. In many communities, teachers can request weekly delivery of free newspapers. However, with the influx of technology, more people get the news from social media and websites such as CNN and *Time*. Student-friendly versions of these news sources include CNN Student News (www.cnn.com /studentnews) and Time for Kids (www.timeforkids.com). Instead of simply watching the clip, answering a few questions, and moving on, it's important for students to deepen their comprehension and worldviews during this activity. Having students use apps such as Lino or Padlet on iPads, tablets, or smartphones fosters a digital conversation while students learn about current events in local and global communities.

While CNN Student News is displayed on the Smart Board, students log into the teacher-created Padlet board, which also displays CNN Student News. Once all students have access to the Padlet board to record digital sticky notes, the teacher can begin the news clip. While students view the news, they record their thoughts, questions, and connections onto the digital canvas. Because students are all on the same board, they can easily see their peers' posts, leading to further discussion and deeper understanding. For example, after a segment on the lack of water in South Sudan, one student posts the question, "What can be done to help people with no water in South Sudan?" Then, one of his classmates states, "My soccer team is collecting money for the Water for South Sudan project." Not only can students discuss world events, they can become activists for social justice.

Make Adaptations

For students who are reluctant to record their thoughts in writing or for students who lack proficiency with typing skills, they may benefit from a verbal approach that still allows them to share their thinking before, during, and after reading. To help build proficiency in typing skills, teachers may want to show students some websites that help build students' familiarity with the keyboard. Sites such as ABCYa.com (www.abcya.com/kids_typing_game.htm) and Bitesize Dance Mat Typing (www.bbc.co.uk/guides/z3c6tfr) offer students practice in learning to type. Until they learn sufficient typing skills, younger students or those with little experience in keyboarding may need to begin with a more traditional approach to recording thinking.

One option to consider when posting stop-and-jots on Lino is to allow students to share their thinking before, during, and after reading using pencil and sticky notes. Then, the student can take a photo of the sticky notes and upload it to his or her Lino boards accordingly. In addition, another option is to allow students to record their thinking using audio or video and then upload it to YouTube or podcasting sites like audioBoom. These links can be embedded within their Lino boards to create a multimodal trail of students' thinking.

UN-CONCLUSION

It's Not the End

One summer evening, enjoying the rare occurrence of one another's company and discussing the layout and content of the book, we started to contemplate the conclusion. Although we typically collaborate in a digital forum and not in person, a substantive, meandering discussion ensued. We covered a great many topics in this discussion, but a significant focus was the ending of our book. *How can we have an ending?* As former elementary school teachers, we remain familiar with the continuous movement of education in general and the ever-changing world of technology, and therefore came to a decision—*we cannot have a conclusion.*

While most books have a concluding chapter or final words, we do not feel as though that would be a good fit for this text. In the words of Donald Murray (1986), we are adding our thoughts on the topic of instructional technology to the "continuous professional conversation" that has been taking place for years and will continue to take place for years to come (p. 147). In *What a Writer Needs, Second Edition*, Ralph Fletcher (2013) writes his *un-final* thoughts in his last chapter. We admire that approach and find it fitting that our book has an *un-conclusion.* Education is a constantly shifting landscape, and with technology, there are always new tools and new possibilities. Therefore, we offer this final chapter of the book as our inconclusive thoughts and to extend the digital tool conversation.

Technology Tools to Foster Learning

Teachers are often miracle workers as they somehow figure out how to teach an impossible number of standards in the little time they have with their students. Technology should not be "one more thing" that teachers have to add to their already jam-packed instructional days. First of all, it may be impossible to squeeze anything else into those few short hours that teachers have with their students. Second, technology can and should be used as a tool to open the classroom to the world, to ensure that teachers present standards in a way that fosters active engagement and participation in meaningful ways.

Technology provides opportunities for students in the realm of creation. Digital tools can also help students to communicate within and beyond the four walls of the classroom (Yearta & Stover, 2015) through the creation of multimodal content and text

(Mills & Levido, 2011). In fact, opportunities for collaboration abound on the Internet (Karchmer-Klein, 2013). Tools such as email, wikis, blogs, the Google suite, and so on can help students to share their thoughts with audiences near and far. Finally, access to digital tools can make it easier for teachers to assess students' work and provide authentic, formative feedback to them.

Tools Change

The digital tools that teachers and students have access to are changing at a rapid pace. When our students started blogging, it was a constant stress to ensure that they were communicating and collaborating in a safe manner. Not much later, student-friendly blogging sites became available, and classrooms could be matched with other classrooms around the world to communicate via a digital platform. While we must remain vigilant when it comes to our students' safety, the digital tools at our fingertips have made it easier to do so. Years ago, our students were setting up tripods with VHS cameras to videotape their reader's theater performances. Now, they grab tablets or smartphones to do the recording and then edit and instantly upload their work to the classroom website from the same device. In this way, parents and peers can view their performances. Although the individual tools are changing, we hope that this book can serve as a framework for rethinking everyday classroom practices in a digital world.

Not only do new tools become available on a daily basis, literacy's very nature is changing as well. In fact, Blanchard and Farstrup (2011) write, "Technology is changing the world we live in—and reading instruction" (p. 306). Adding to that sentiment, Leu and his colleagues write that "literacy is now deictic" (Leu et al., 2011, p. 6). A deictic concept is dependent on context. Therefore, when we say that we want our students to be literate, it is important to know that the concept of *being literate* is a moving target. What it means to be literate today is different than what it meant to be literate yesterday, and it will be different tomorrow.

Shifts in Education

Michele Knobel and Colin Lankshear (2014) discuss the way in which the very nature of education continuously shifts. Traditional schooling involved the teacher as the keeper of knowledge. Books held the information that students needed. Texts were used year after year, and that information remained finite. In the 21st century, information is updated and readily available in real time. As teachers, we no longer need to be the gatekeepers of knowledge. Rather, we must teach our students how to be critical consumers of the available information and producers of information (Anstey & Bull, 2006; Leu, Zawilinski, Forzani, & Timbrell, 2015).

In order to be competitive in the global market, our students cannot simply consume information. Gone are the days when students receptively sat and listened to lectures. Now, students must create, revise, communicate with others, collaborate on projects, and solicit and receive feedback from other experts in the field (Knobel & Lankshear, 2014). Technology can be integrated to "support the broader, higher level, and more important aspects of literacy—namely, critical thinking, judgment, problem-solving skills, and development of lifelong reading and thinking habits" (Blanchard & Farstrup, 2011, p. 304).

Teachers as Lifelong Learners

To compete and participate in the new global society, students need opportunities to ask genuine and reflective questions, to collaborate, to create, and to communicate their learning and ideas. Using technology as a tool in the classroom is clearly a vital part of fulfilling that need, but how do we, as educators, get started and stay relevant in this process? Rather than experimenting with every tool in this book at once, we suggest you begin by exploring one tool and the possible ways you might implement it.

In Ralph Fletcher's (2013) last chapter, he implores his readers to explore, to live, to try new things. He writes, "Real exploration means that you'll probably get lost. That's all right" (p. 178). Try a new technology tool. As educators, we should know what it is like to try a new digital tool, to participate in something greater than ourselves (Knobel & Lankshear, 2014). You will most likely struggle. You will probably get frustrated. It will be OK. It is through the struggle that we learn. Additionally, the struggle provides you with thoughts and ideas to share with your students when you ask that they compile a digital portfolio or tweet about their science explorations with other third graders across the country. In this way, the technological tool authentically becomes a part of the students' repertoire and your own. As you begin or continue your professional journey in the digital world, feel free to share with us some of the tools that you have found useful. We can be reached on Twitter @KStover24 and @LYearta. We look forward to the continued conversation.

Katie and Lindsay

APPENDIX

Reproducibles

Research Template

Students can use the following template to brainstorm ideas for a research project.

Topic: _____

After spending at least one hour reading through texts, write some interesting facts that you found. Don't forget to include where you found the information!

Interesting fact:	Where I found the interesting fact:
Interesting fact:	Where I found the interesting fact:
Interesting fact:	Where I found the interesting fact:

1. Summarize what you have learned in one sentence. So far, I have learned:

    _____

    _____

    _____

    _____

    _____

2. Write at least two questions you still have:

_____

_____

_____

_____

_____

3. Where might you find the answers to those questions?

_____

_____

_____

_____

_____

Scaffolded Reflection Questions

When reflecting on your reading history, consider the following questions to scaffold this process. Based on your responses, determine possible goals for yourself as a reader.

1. What was the first book you remember someone reading to you?

   _____

2. What did you think about that book?

   _____

3. What is the first book you remember reading on your own?

   _____

4. What did you think about that book?

   _____

5. What other books do you remember reading?

   _____

6. Why did you choose those books?

   _____

7. Did you finish them? Why or why not?

   _____

8. What books have your teachers read to you?

   _____

9. Did you enjoy listening to those books? Why or why not?

   _____

10. Do your friends recommend books for you to read?

   _____

11. What other items do you spend time reading? Why?

   _____

12. What do you remember about reading at home?

   _____

13. What do you remember about reading at school?

   _____

References and Resources

Abodeeb-Gentile, T., & Zawilinski, L. (2013). Reader identity and the Common Core: Agency and identity in leveled reading. *Language and Literacy Spectrum, 23*, 34–45.

Abrami, P. C., & Barrett, H. (2005). Directions for research and development on electronic portfolios. *Canadian Journal of Learning and Technology, 31*(3), 1–15.

Afflerbach, P., Cho, B.-Y., Kim, J.-Y., Crassas, M. E., & Doyle, B. (2013). Reading: What else matters besides strategies and skills? *The Reading Teacher, 66*(6), 440–448.

Allen, J. (2007). *Creating welcoming schools: A practical guide to home-school partnerships with diverse families.* New York: Teachers College Press.

Allington, R. L. (2012). *What really matters for struggling readers: Designing research-based programs* (3rd ed.). Boston: Pearson.

Allington, R. L. (2013). What really matters when working with struggling readers. *The Reading Teacher, 66*(7), 520–530.

Allington, R. L., & Gabriel, R. E. (2012). Every child, every day. *Educational Leadership, 69*(6), 10–15.

Anderson, C. (2000). *How's it going?: A practical guide to conferring with student writers.* Portsmouth, NH: Heinemann.

Anderson, C. (2005). *Assessing writers.* Portsmouth, NH: Heinemann.

Anderson, R. C., & Freebody, P. (1981). Vocabulary knowledge. In J. T. Guthrie (Ed.), *Comprehension and teaching: Research reviews* (pp. 77–117). Newark, DE: International Reading Association.

Angelillo, J. (2005). *Making revision matter.* New York: Scholastic.

Anstey, M., & Bull, G. (2006). *Teaching and learning multiliteracies: Changing times, changing literacies.* Newark, DE: International Reading Association.

Applegate, K. (2007). *Home of the brave.* New York: Macmillan.

Axelrod, Y. (2014). Images and text: Learning "beyond and within our four walls." *Reading Matters, 14*, 51–53.

Bandura, A. (1977). *Social learning theory.* New York: General Learning Press.

Barone, D. M., & Mallette, M. H. (2013). On using Twitter. *The Reading Teacher, 66*(5), 377–379.

Bates, C. C. (2013). How do *Wii* know?: Anecdotal records go digital. *The Reading Teacher*, *67*(1), 25–29.

Baumann, J. F., Edwards, E. C., Font, G., Tereshinski, C. A., Kame'enui, E. J., & Olejnik, S. (2002). Teaching morphemic and contextual analysis to fifth-grade students. *Reading Research Quarterly*, *37*(2), 150–176.

Beach, R., & Lundell, D. (1998). Early adolescents' use of computer-mediated communication in writing and reading. In D. Reinking, M. C. McKenna, L. D. Labbo, & R. D. Kieffer (Eds.), *Handbook of literacy and technology: Transformations in a post-typographic world* (pp. 102–123). Mahwah, NJ: Erlbaum.

Bear, D. R., Invernizzi, M., Templeton, S., & Johnston, F. (2012). *Words their way: Word study for phonics, vocabulary, and spelling instruction* (5th ed.). Boston: Pearson.

Beck, I. L., McKeown, M. G., & Kucan, L. (2002). *Bringing words to life: Robust vocabulary instruction*. New York: Guilford Press.

Becker, W. (n.d.). *Underground railroad*. Accessed at www.tes.com/lessons/SX9U-zWCcuex4g /underground-railroad?redirect-bs=1 on March 10, 2016.

Beers, K. (2003). *When kids can't read, what teachers can do: A guide for teachers 6–12*. Portsmouth, NH: Heinemann.

Biemiller, A. (2001). Teaching vocabulary: Early, direct, and sequential. *American Educator*, *25*(1), 24–28, 47.

Biemiller, A., & Boote, C. (2006). An effective method for building meaning vocabulary in primary grades. *Journal of Educational Psychology*, *98*(1), 44–62.

Blachowicz, C. Z., & Fisher, P. J. (2006). *Teaching vocabulary in all classrooms* (3rd ed.). Upper Saddle River, NJ: Pearson/Merrill Prentice Hall.

Blanchard, J. S., & Farstrup, A. E. (2011). Technologies, digital media, and reading instruction. In S. J. Samuels & A. E. Farstrup (Eds.), *What research has to say about reading instruction* (4th ed., pp. 286–314). Newark, DE: International Reading Association.

Bogard, J. M., & McMackin, M. C. (2012). Combining traditional and new literacies in a 21st-century writing workshop. *The Reading Teacher*, *65*(5), 313–323.

Boling, E., Castek, J., Zawilinski, L., Barton, K., & Nierlich, T. (2008). Collaborative literacy: Blogs and Internet projects. *The Reading Teacher*, *61*(6), 504–506.

Boyd-Batstone, P. (2004). Focused anecdotal records assessment: A tool for standards-based, authentic assessment. *The Reading Teacher*, *58*(3), 230–239.

Brett, J. (1989). *The mitten: A Ukrainian folktale*. New York: Putnam.

Britton, J. (1971). *Language and learning*. New York: Penguin.

Brown, M. W. (1999). *The important book*. New York: HarperCollins.

Bruce, B. C., & Rubin, A. (1993). *Electronic quills: A situated evaluation of using computers for writing in classrooms*. Hillsdale, NJ: Erlbaum.

Bunting, E. (1998). *So far from the sea*. New York: Clarion Books.

Bunyi, A. (2010, November 5). *Identifying reliable sources and citing them.* Accessed at www .scholastic.com/teachers/top-teaching/2010/11/reliable-sources-and-citations on March 10, 2016.

Burley, H., & Price, M. (2003). What works with authentic assessment. *Educational Horizons, 81*(4), 193–196.

Calkins, L. M. (1994). *The art of teaching writing* (New ed.). Portsmouth, NH: Heinemann.

Carico, K., & Logan, D. (2004). A generation in cyberspace engaging readers through online discussions. *Language Arts, 81*(4), 293–302.

Carlsen, G. R., & Sherrill, A. (1988). *Voices of readers: How we come to love books.* Urbana, IL: National Council of Teachers of English.

Casbergue, R. M. (2011). Assessment and instruction in early childhood education: Early literacy as a microcosm of shifting perspectives. *Journal of Education, 190*(1/2), 13–20.

Cazden, C. B. (1988). *Classroom discourse: The language of teaching and learning.* Portsmouth, NH: Heinemann.

Chard, D. J., Vaughn, S., & Tyler, B.-J. (2002). A synthesis of research on effective interventions for building reading fluency with elementary students with learning disabilities. *Journal of Learning Disabilities, 35*(5), 386–406.

Civil and political rights. (n.d.). In *Wikipedia.* Accessed at https://en.wikipedia.org/wiki /Civil_and_political_rights on December 10, 2015.

Cohen, V. L., & Cowen, J. E. (2011). *Literacy for children in an information age: Teaching reading, writing, and thinking* (2nd ed.). Belmont, CA: Wadsworth.

Coiro, J. (2003a). Reading comprehension on the Internet: Expanding our understanding of reading comprehension to encompass new literacies. *The Reading Teacher, 56*(5), 458–464.

Coiro, J. (2003b). Rethinking comprehension strategies to better prepare students for critically evaluating content on the Internet. *New England Reading Association Journal, 39*(2), 29–34.

Coiro, J. (2014, April 7). *Teaching adolescents how to evaluate the quality of online information* [Blog post]. Accessed at www.edutopia.org/blog/evaluating-quality-of-online-info-julie-coiro on July 20, 2015.

Coiro, J., Castek, J., & Guzniczak, L. (2011). Uncovering online reading comprehension processes: Two adolescents reading independently and collaboratively on the Internet. In P. J. Dunston, L. B. Gambrell, K. Headley, S. K. Fullerton, P. M. Stecker, V. R. Gillis, et al. (Eds.), *60th yearbook of the Literacy Research Association* (pp. 354–369). Oak Creek, WI: Literacy Research Association.

Cruz, M. C. (2008). *A quick guide to reading struggling writers, K–5.* Portsmouth, NH: Heinemann.

Cunningham, A. E., & Stanovich, K. E. (1997). Early reading acquisition and its relation to reading experience and ability 10 years later. *Developmental Psychology, 33*(6), 934–945.

Dalton, B. (2012). Multimodal composition and the Common Core State Standards. *The Reading Teacher, 66*(4), 333–339.

Dean, D. (2000). Going public: Letters to the world. *Voices From the Middle, 8*(1), 42–47.

dePaola, T. (1979). *Oliver Button is a sissy.* New York: Harcourt Brace Jovanovich.

Derrick3RD. (n.d.). Nia the Night Owl Fairy *book review* [Podcast]. Accessed at https://audioboom .com/boos/2723166-nia-the-night-owl-fairy-book-review on March 10, 2016.

Dobler, E. (2011/2012). Using iPads to promote literacy in the primary grades. *Reading Today, 29*(3), 18–19.

Dorfman, L. R., & Cappelli, R. (2009). *Nonfiction mentor texts: Teaching informational writing through children's literature, K–8.* Portland, ME: Stenhouse.

Draper, S. M. (2012). *Out of my mind.* New York: Atheneum Books for Young Readers.

Dudley-Marling, C., & Paugh, P. (2004). *A classroom teacher's guide to struggling readers.* Portsmouth, NH: Heinemann.

Dudley-Marling, C., & Paugh, P. (2009). *A classroom teacher's guide to struggling writers: How to provide differentiated support and ongoing assessment.* Portsmouth, NH: Heinemann.

Eagleton, M. B., & Guinee, K. (2002). Strategies for supporting student Internet inquiry. *New England Reading Association Journal, 38*(2), 39–47.

Eagleton, M. B., Guinee, K., & Langlais, K. (2003). Teaching Internet literacy strategies: The hero inquiry project. *Voices From the Middle, 10*(3), 28–35.

Easel.ly. (2014). *About us.* Accessed at www.easel.ly/blog/about-us on February 15, 2016.

Eccles-Parsons, J. S., Adler, T. F., Futterman, R., Goff, S. B., Kaczala, C. M., Meece, J. L., et al. (1983). Expectancies, values, and academic behaviors. In J. T. Spence (Ed.), *Achievement and achievement motives: Psychological and sociological approaches* (pp. 75–146). San Francisco: Freeman.

Edutopia. (2008, March 16). *Why integrate technology into the curriculum?: The reasons are many.* Accessed at www.edutopia.org/technology-integration-introduction on July 20, 2015.

Ferriter, W. M. (2010). Digitally speaking: Why teachers should try Twitter. *Educational Leadership, 67*(5), 73–74. Accessed at www.ascd.org/publications/educational-leadership/feb10/vol67 /num05/Why-Teachers-Should-Try-Twitter.aspx on December 19, 2014.

Fiene, J., & McMahon, S. (2007). Assessing comprehension: A classroom-based process. *The Reading Teacher, 60*(5), 406–417.

Fisher, D., & Frey, N. (2009). Feed up, back, forward. *Educational Leadership, 67*(3), 20–25.

Fletcher, R. (2013). *What a writer needs* (2nd ed.). Portsmouth, NH: Heinemann.

Fletcher, R., & Portalupi, J. (2001). *Writing workshop: The essential guide.* Portsmouth, NH: Heinemann.

Fountas, I. C., & Pinnell, G. S. (2001). *Guiding readers and writers, grades 3–6: Teaching comprehension, genre, and content literacy.* Portsmouth, NH: Heinemann.

Fox, M. (1990). *Mem's the word.* New York: Penguin.

Fox, M. (1994). *Tough Boris.* Orlando, FL: Harcourt Brace.

Gabriel, R., & Gabriel, M. (2010). Power in pictures: How a schoolwide photo library can build a community of readers and writers. *The Reading Teacher, 63*(8), 679–682.

Gabriel, T. (2010, October 26). Generation plagiarism? *New York Times Upfront,* vol. 143. Accessed at http://teacher.scholastic.com/scholasticnews/indepth/upfront/features/index.asp ?article=f102510_plagiarism on August 13, 2015.

Gambrell, L. B. (1996). Creating classroom cultures that foster reading motivation. *The Reading Teacher, 50*(1), 14–25.

Gambrell, L. B. (2011). Seven rules of engagement: What's most important to know about motivation to read. *The Reading Teacher, 65*(3), 172–178.

Garner, R., & Gillingham, M. G. (1996). *Internet communication in six classrooms: Conversations across time, space, and culture.* Mahwah, NJ: Erlbaum.

Garner, R., & Gillingham, M. G. (1998). The Internet in the classroom: Is it the end of transmission-oriented pedagogy? In D. Reinking, M. C. McKenna, L. D. Labbo, & R. D. Kieffer (Eds.), *Handbook of literacy and technology: Transformations in a post-typographic world* (pp. 245–257). Mahwah, NJ: Erlbaum.

Graham, S., & Harris, K. R. (2013). Designing an effective writing program. In S. Graham, C. A. MacArthur, & J. Fitzgerald (Eds.), *Best practices in writing instruction* (2nd ed., pp. 3–25). New York: Guilford Press.

Graves, D. H. (1983). *Writing: Teachers and children at work.* Exeter, NH: Heinemann Educational Books.

Graves, M. F. (2009). *Teaching individual words: One size does not fit all.* New York: Teachers College Press.

Graves, M. F., & Watts-Taffe, S. M. (2002). The place of word consciousness in a research-based vocabulary program. In A. E. Farstrup & S. J. Samuels (Eds.), *What research has to say about reading instruction* (3rd ed., pp. 140–165). Newark, DE: International Reading Association.

Griffith, L. W., & Rasinski, T. V. (2004). A focus on fluency: How one teacher incorporated fluency with her reading curriculum. *The Reading Teacher, 58*(2), 126–137.

Grisham, D. L., & Wolsey, T. D. (2006). Recentering the middle school classroom as a vibrant learning community: Students, literacy, and technology intersect. *Journal of Adolescent and Adult Literacy, 49*(8), 648–660.

Guinee, K., Eagleton, M. B., & Hall, T. E. (2003). Adolescents' Internet search strategies: Drawing upon familiar cognitive paradigms when accessing electronic information sources. *Journal of Educational Computing Research, 29*(3), 363–374.

Gulf Coast State College Library. (2013, February 12). *Evaluating websites* [Video file]. Accessed at https://youtu.be/aem3JahbXfk on February 26, 2016.

Guthrie, J. T., & Wigfield, A. (2000). Engagement and motivation in reading. In M. L. Kamil, P. B. Mosenthal, P. D. Pearson, & R. Barr (Eds.), *Handbook of reading research* (Vol. 3, pp. 403–422). Mahwah, NJ: Erlbaum.

Guthrie, J. T., Wigfield, A., & You, W. (2012). Instructional contexts for engagement and achievement in reading. In S. L. Christenson, A. L. Reschly, & C. Wylie (Eds.), *Handbook of research on student engagement* (pp. 601–634). New York: Springer.

Haggard, M. R. (1986). The vocabulary self-collection strategy: Using student interest and world knowledge to enhance vocabulary growth. *Journal of Reading, 29*(7), 634–642.

Hansen, J. A. (2007). First grade writers revisit their work. *Young Children, 62*(1), 28–33.

156 | FROM PENCILS TO PODCASTS

Harmon, J. M., Wood, K. D., Hedrick, W. B., & Gress, M. (2008). "Pick a word—not just any word": Using vocabulary self-selection with expository texts. *Middle School Journal, 40*(1), 43–52.

Harmon, J. M., Wood, K. D., & Kiser, K. (2009). Promoting vocabulary learning with the interactive word wall. *Middle School Journal, 40*(3), 58–63.

Hart, B., & Risley, R. T. (1995). *Meaningful differences in the everyday experience of young American children.* Baltimore: Brookes.

Harvey, S., & Goudvis, A. (2007). *Strategies that work: Teaching comprehension for understanding and engagement* (2nd ed.). Portland, ME: Stenhouse.

Heard, G. (2002). *The revision toolbox: Teaching techniques that work.* Portsmouth, NH: Heinemann.

Hearne, B. (1997). *Seven brave women.* New York: Greenwillow Books.

Henry, L. A. (2006). SEARCHing for an answer: The critical role of new literacies while reading on the Internet. *The Reading Teacher, 59*(7), 614–627.

Heritage, M. (2010, September). *Formative assessment and next-generation assessment systems: Are we losing an opportunity?* Washington, DC: Council of Chief State School Officers. Accessed at www.ccsso.org/Documents/2010/Formative_Assessment_Next_Generation_2010.pdf on July 17, 2015.

Hindley, J. (1996). *In the company of children.* Portland, ME: Stenhouse.

Hoffert, B. (2010). Every reader a reviewer: The online book conversation. *Library Journal, 135*(14), 22–25.

Hoffman, J. L. (2011). Coconstructing meaning: Interactive literary discussions in kindergarten read-alouds. *The Reading Teacher, 65*(3), 183–194.

International Literacy Association. (2001). *Integrating literacy and technology in the curriculum* [Position statement]. Newark, DE: Author. Accessed at www.literacyworldwide.org/docs/default-source/where-we-stand/technology-position-statement.pdf?sfvrsn=6 on March 30, 2016.

International Literacy Association. (2009). *New literacies and 21st-century technologies: A position statement of the International Reading Association.* Newark, DE: Author.

International Literacy Association. (2013). *Formative assessment: A position statement of the International Reading Association.* Newark, DE: Author.

International Reading Association & National Council of Teachers of English. (1996). *Standards for the English language arts.* Newark, DE: Authors. Accessed at www.ncte.org/library/NCTEFiles/Resources/Books/Sample/StandardsDoc.pdf on February 15, 2016.

International Society for Technology in Education. (2007). *ISTE standards for students.* Accessed at www.iste.org/standards/ISTE-standards/standards-for-students on August 16, 2015.

International Society for Technology in Education. (2008). *ISTE standards for teachers.* Accessed at www.iste.org/docs/pdfs/20-14_ISTE_Standards-T_PDF.pdf on January 14, 2016.

Jackson, J., & Narvaez, R. (2013). Interactive word walls: Create a tool to increase science vocabulary in five easy steps. *Science and Children, 51*(1), 42–49.

Kara-Soteriou, J., & Callan, A. (2014). Digital storytelling. In R. E. Ferdig, T. V. Rasinski, & K. E. Pytash (Eds.), *Using technology to enhance writing: Innovative approaches to literacy instruction* (pp. 79–85). Bloomington, IN: Solution Tree Press.

Karchmer-Klein, R. (2013). Best practices in using technology to support writing. In S. Graham, C. A. MacArthur, & J. Fitzgerald (Eds.), *Best practices in writing instruction* (2nd ed., pp. 309–333). New York: Guilford Press.

Karchmer-Klein, R., & Shinas, V. H. (2012). Guiding principles for supporting new literacies in your classroom. *The Reading Teacher, 65*(5), 288–293.

Kear, D. J., Coffman, G. A., McKenna, M. C., & Ambrosio, A. L. (2000). Measuring attitude toward writing: A new tool for teachers. *The Reading Teacher, 54*(1), 10–23.

Kellner, D., & Share, J. (2007). Critical media literacy, democracy, and the reconstruction of education. In D. Macedo & S. R. Steinberg (Eds.), *Media literacy: A reader* (pp. 3–23). New York: Peter Lang.

Kiili, C., Laurinen, L., Marttunen, M., & Leu, D. J. (2012). Working on understanding during collaborative online reading. *Journal of Literacy Research, 44*(4), 448–483.

Kiili, C., Makinen, M., & Coiro, J. (2013). Rethinking academic literacies: Designing multifaceted academic literacy experiences for preservice teachers. *Journal of Adolescent and Adult Literacy, 57*(3), 223–232.

Kissel, B., Miller, E., & Hansen, J. (2015). Writers' workshop: Using retro ideas to re-envision student-led agendas. In K. D. Wood, J. R. Paratore, B. Kissel, & R. McCormack (Eds.), *What's new in literacy teaching?: Weaving together time-honored practices with new research* (pp. 82–94). Newark, DE: International Literacy Association.

Kissel, B., Putman, S. M., & Stover, K. (2013). Using digital portfolios to enhance students' capacity for communication about learning. In K. E. Pytash & R. E. Ferdig (Eds.), *Exploring technology for writing and writing instruction* (pp. 37–53). Hershey, PA: IGI Global.

Klein, P. D., & Yu, A. M. (2013). Best practices in writing to learn. In S. Graham, C. A. MacArthur, & J. Fitzgerald (Eds.), *Best practices in writing instruction* (2nd ed., pp. 166–189). New York: Guilford Press.

Knipper, K. J., & Duggan, T. J. (2006). Writing to learn across the curriculum: Tools for comprehension in content area classes. *The Reading Teacher, 59*(5), 462–470.

Knobel, M., & Lankshear, C. (2014). Studying new literacies. *Journal of Adolescent and Adult Literacy, 58*(2), 97–101.

Knobel, M., & Wilber, D. (2009). Let's talk 2.0. *Educational Leadership, 66*(6), 20–24.

Korman, G. (2012). *Ungifted.* New York: HarperCollins.

Kress, G. (2010). *Multimodality: A social semiotic approach to contemporary communication.* New York: Routledge.

Krieger, E. (1991/1992). The book report battle (from the teacher's desk). *Journal of Reading, 35*(4), 340–341.

Laidlaw, L. (1998). Finding "real" lives: Writing and identity. *Language Arts, 75*(2), 126–131.

Lankshear, C., & Knobel, M. (2003). *New literacies: Changing knowledge and classroom learning.* Maidenhead, England: Open University Press.

Lankshear, C., & Knobel, M. (2006). *New literacies: Everyday practices and classroom learning* (2nd ed.). Maidenhead, England: Open University Press.

Larkin, K., & Finger, G. (2011). Informing one-to-one computing in primary schools: Student use of netbooks. *Australasian Journal of Educational Technology, 27*(3), 514–530.

Larson, L. C. (2009). Reader response meets new literacies: Empowering readers in online learning communities. *The Reading Teacher, 62*(8), 638–648.

Laru, J., Naykki, P., & Jarvela, S. (2012). Supporting small-group learning using multiple web 2.0 tools: A case study in the higher education context. *The Internet and Higher Education, 15*(1), 29–38.

Lensmire, T. J. (1992, November 23). *Peers, risk and writing.* Paper presented at the annual meeting of the National Reading Conference, San Antonio, TX.

Lenters, K., & Winters, K.-L. (2013). Fracturing writing spaces: Multimodal storytelling ignites process writing. *The Reading Teacher, 67*(3), 227–237.

Leu, D. J. (2000). Our children's future: Changing the focus of literacy and literacy instruction. *The Reading Teacher, 53*(5), 424–431.

Leu, D. J. (2002). The new literacies: Research on reading instruction with the Internet. In A. E. Farstrup & S. J. Samuels (Eds.), *What research has to say about reading instruction* (3rd ed., pp. 310–336). Newark, DE: International Reading Association.

Leu, D. J., Kinzer, C. K., Coiro, J., & Cammack, D. W. (2004). Toward a theory of new literacies emerging from the Internet and other communication technologies. In R. B. Ruddell & N. J. Unrau (Eds.), *Theoretical models and processes of reading* (5th ed., pp. 1570–1613). Newark, DE: International Reading Association.

Leu, D. J., McVerry, J. G., O'Byrne, W. I., Kiili, C., Zawilinski, L., Everett-Cacopardo, H., et al. (2011). The new literacies of online reading comprehension: Expanding the literacy and learning curriculum. *Journal of Adolescent and Adult Literacy, 55*(1), 5–14.

Leu, D. J., Zawilinski, L., Forzani, E., & Timbrell, N. (2015). Best practices in teaching the new literacies of online research and comprehension. In L. B. Gambrell & L. M. Morrow (Eds.), *Best practices in literacy instruction* (5th ed., pp. 343–364). New York: Guilford Press.

Litwin, E. (2010). *Pete the cat: I love my white shoes.* New York: HarperCollins.

Long, M. (2003). *How I became a pirate.* Orlando, FL: Harcourt Brace.

Mandell, S., Sorge, D. H., & Russell, J. D. (2002). TIPs for technology integration. *TechTrends: Linking Research and Practice to Improve Learning, 46*(5), 39–43.

Manyak, P. C., Von Gunten, H., Autenrieth, D., Gillis, C., Mastre-O'Farrell, J., Irvine-McDermott, E., et al. (2014). Four practical principles for enhancing vocabulary instruction. *The Reading Teacher, 68*(1), 13–23.

Martens, P., Martens, R., Doyle, M. H., Loomis, J., & Aghalarov, S. (2012). Learning from picturebooks: Reading and writing multimodally in first grade. *The Reading Teacher, 66*(4), 285–294.

Martinez, M., Roser, N. L., & Strecker, S. (1998/1999). "I never thought I could be a star": A reader's theatre ticket to fluency. *The Reading Teacher, 52*(4), 326–334.

McCabe, P. (2009). Enhancing adolescent self-efficacy for literacy. In K. D. Wood & W. E. Blanton (Eds.), *Literacy instruction for adolescents: Research-based practice* (pp. 54–76). New York: Guilford Press.

McCormick, K. (2010, September). Experiencing the power of learning mathematics through writing. *Issues in the Undergraduate Mathematics Preparation of School Teachers, 4,* 1–8.

McKenna, M. C., & Stahl, K. A. D. (2009). *Assessment for reading instruction* (2nd ed.). New York: Guilford Press.

McNair, S., Bhargava, A., Adams, L., Edgerton, S., & Kypros, B. (2003). Teachers speak out on assessment practices. *Early Childhood Education Journal, 31*(1), 23–31.

Meadows, D. (2011). *Nia the night owl fairy.* New York: Scholastic.

Merchant, G. (2005). Electronic involvement: Identify performance in children's informal digital writing. *Discourse: Studies in the Cultural Politics of Education, 26*(3), 301–314.

Merkley, D., Schmidt, D., Dirksen, C., & Fuhler, C. (2006). Enhancing parent-teacher communication using technology: A reading improvement clinic example. *Contemporary Issues in Technology and Teacher Education, 6*(1), 11–42.

Messner, K. (2009). Pleased to tweet you: Making a case for Twitter in the classroom. *School Library Journal, 55*(12), 44–47. Accessed at http://webtools4teachers.yolasite.com/resources/Pleased +to+Tweet+You+Making+a+case+for+Twitter+in+the+Classroom.pdf on December 19, 2014.

Metzger, S. (2013). *Lincoln and Grace: Why Abraham Lincoln grew a beard.* New York: Scholastic.

Mills, K. A., & Levido, A. (2011). iPed: Pedagogy for digital text production. *The Reading Teacher, 65*(1), 80–91.

Mixan, M. (2013). In-depth study of vocabulary development. *Reading Improvement, 50*(3), 118–120.

Mochizuki, K. (1993). *Baseball saved us.* New York: Scholastic.

Moll, L. C., Amanti, C., Neff, D., & Gonzalez, N. (1992). Funds of knowledge for teaching: Using a qualitative approach to connect homes and classrooms. *Theory Into Practice, 31*(2), 132–141.

Moore, M. E. (2014, June 13). *Promoting a collaborative environment with classroom blogs* [Blog post]. Accessed at http://literacyworldwide.org/blog/literacy-daily/2014/06/13/promoting-a -collaborative-environment-with-classroom-blogs on March 2, 2016.

Morrow, L. M. (1996). Story retelling: A discussion strategy to develop and assess comprehension. In L. B. Gambrell & J. F. Almasi (Eds.), *Lively discussions!: Fostering engaged reading* (pp. 265–285). Newark, DE: International Reading Association.

Mraz, M., & Rasinski, T. V. (2007). Summer reading loss. *The Reading Teacher, 60*(8), 784–789.

Murray, D. M. (1986). One writer's secrets. *College Composition and Communication, 37*(2), 146–153.

Murray, D. M. (1999a). How to get the writing done. In W. Bishop (Ed.), *The subject is writing: Essays by teachers and students* (2nd ed., pp. 55–61). Portsmouth, NH: Boynton/Cook.

Murray, D. M. (1999b). *Write to learn* (6th ed.). Fort Worth, TX: Harcourt Brace College.

Myers, J., Hammett, R., & McKillop, A. M. (1998). Opportunities for critical literacy and pedagogy in student-authored hypermedia. In D. Reinking, M. C. McKenna, L. D. Labbo, & R. D. Kieffer (Eds.), *Handbook of literacy and technology: Transformations in a post-typographic world* (pp. 67–84). Mahwah, NJ: Erlbaum.

National Council of Teachers of English. (2005, November). *Position statement on multimodal literacies.* Urbana, IL: Author. Accessed at www.ncte.org/positions/statements/multimodalliteracies on December 7, 2015.

National Early Literacy Panel. (2008). *Developing early literacy: Report of the National Early Literacy Panel—A scientific synthesis of early literacy development and implications for intervention.* Washington, DC: National Institute for Literacy.

National Governors Association Center for Best Practices & Council of Chief State School Officers. (2010). *Common Core State Standards for English language arts and literacy in history/social studies, science, and technical subjects.* Washington, DC: Authors. Accessed at www.corestandards.org/assets/CCSSI_ELA%20Standards.pdf on December 7, 2015.

National Reading Panel. (2000, April). *Teaching children to read: An evidence-based assessment of the scientific research literature on reading and its implications for reading instruction—Reports of the subgroups* (NIH Pub. No. 00-4769). Washington, DC: National Institute of Child Health and Human Development. Accessed at www.nichd.nih.gov/publications/pubs/nrp/documents/report.pdf on August 2, 2016.

Newell, G. E., VanDerHeide, J., & Wilson, M. (2013). Best practices in teaching informative writing from sources. In S. Graham, C. A. MacArthur, & J. Fitzgerald (Eds.), *Best practices in writing instruction* (2nd ed., pp. 141–165). New York: Guilford Press.

New London Group. (1996). A pedagogy of multiliteracies: Designing social futures. *Harvard Educational Review, 66*(1), 60–92.

Northrop, L., & Killeen, E. (2013). A framework for using iPads to build early literacy skills. *The Reading Teacher, 66*(7), 531–537.

Ohler, J. (2005/2006). The world of digital storytelling. *Educational Leadership, 63*(4), 44–47.

O'Reilly, T. (2005, September 30). *What is web 2.0: Design patterns and business models for the next generation of software.* Accessed at http://oreilly.com/web2/archive/what-is-web-20.html on December 7, 2015.

Paratore, J. R. (2011). Parents and reading: What teachers should know about ways to support productive home-school environments. In S. J. Samuels & A. E. Farstrup (Eds.), *What research has to say about reading instruction* (4th ed., pp. 406–424). Newark, DE: International Reading Association.

Park, S. W. (2013). The potential of web 2.0 tools to promote reading engagement in a general education course. *TechTrends: Linking Research and Practice to Improve Learning, 57*(2), 46–53.

Paterson, K. (1977). *Bridge to Terabithia.* New York: HarperCollins.

Peebles, J. L. (2007). Incorporating movement with fluency instruction: A motivation for struggling readers. *The Reading Teacher, 60*(6), 578–581.

Perkins, S., & Saltsman, G. (2010). Mobile learning at Abilene Christian University: Successes, challenges, and results from year one. *Journal of the Research Center for Educational Technology*, *6*(1), 47–54.

Rasinski, T. V. (2006). Reading fluency instruction: Moving beyond accuracy, automaticity, and prosody. *The Reading Teacher*, *59*(7), 704–706.

Rasinski, T. V., Padak, N., Newton, J., & Newton, E. (2011). The Latin-Greek connection: Building vocabulary through morphological study. *The Reading Teacher*, *65*(2), 133–141.

Reinking, D., & Watkins, J. (2000). A formative experiment investigating the use of multimedia book reviews to increase elementary students' independent reading. *Reading Research Quarterly*, *35*(3), 384–419.

Rhodes, J. (2013, March 22). *TILE-SIG feature: Resources for teaching critical evaluation of online information* [Blog post]. Accessed at http://literacyworldwide.org/blog/literacy-daily/2013/03/22/tile-sig-feature-resources-for-teaching-critical-evaluation-of-online-information on March 10, 2016.

Rosenblatt, L. M. (1978). *The reader, the text, the poem: The transactional theory of the literary work.* Carbondale, IL: Southern Illinois University Press.

Roskos, K., & Neuman, S. B. (2012). Formative assessment: Simply, no additives. *The Reading Teacher*, *65*(8), 534–538.

Sandvick, M., Smørdal, O., & Østerud, S. (2012). Exploring iPads in practitioners' repertoires for language learning and literacy practices in kindergarten. *Nordic Journal of Digital Literacy*, *7*(3), 204–220.

Scieszka, J., & Smith, L. (1992). *The stinky cheese man and other fairly stupid tales.* New York: Viking.

Seeger, V., & Johnson, R. D. (2014). Electronic family message journals. In R. E. Ferdig, T. V. Rasinski, & K. E. Pytash (Eds.), *Using technology to enhance writing: Innovative approaches to literacy instruction* (pp. 99–104). Bloomington, IN: Solution Tree Press.

Shanahan, T. (2013). Best practices in writing about text. In S. Graham, C. A. MacArthur, & J. Fitzgerald (Eds.), *Best practices in writing instruction* (2nd ed., pp. 334–350). New York: Guilford Press.

Sipe, L. R. (2008). *Storytime: Young children's literary understanding in the classroom.* New York: Teachers College Press.

Skerrett, A. (2012). "We hatched in this class": Repositioning of identity in and beyond a reading classroom. *High School Journal*, *95*(3), 62–75.

Solomon, G., & Schrum, L. (2007). *Web 2.0: New tools, new schools.* Washington, DC: International Society for Technology in Education.

Stover, K., Kissel, B., Wood, K., & Putman, M. (2015). Examining literacy teachers' perceptions of the use of VoiceThread in an elementary, middle school, and a high school classroom for enhancing instructional goals. *Literacy Research and Instruction*, *54*(4), 341–362.

Stover, K., Sparrow, A., & Siefert, B. (2016). "It ain't hard no more!": Individualizing instruction for struggling readers. *Preventing School Failure: Alternative Education for Children and Youth*, 1–10.

Stover, K., & Yearta, L. S. (2015). Using blogs as formative assessment of reading comprehension. In T. V. Rasinski, K. E. Pytash, & R. E. Ferdig. (Eds.), *Using technology to enhance reading: Innovative approaches to literacy instruction* (pp. 223–232). Bloomington, IN: Solution Tree Press.

Stover, K., Yearta, L. S., & Harris, C. (2016). Experiential learning for preservice teachers: Digital book clubs with third graders. *Journal of Digital Learning in Teacher Education*, *32*(1), 5–12.

Stover, K., & Young, C. (2014). Using 21st century technology to edit and revise. In R. E. Ferdig., T. V. Rasinski, & K. E. Pytash (Eds.), *Using technology to enhance writing: Innovative approaches to literacy instruction* (pp. 185–192). Bloomington, IN: Solution Tree Press.

Strickland, D. S., Morrow, L. M., Neuman, S. B., Roskos, K., Schickedanz, J. A., & Vukelich, C. (2004). The role of literacy in early childhood education. *The Reading Teacher*, *58*(1), 86–100.

Strickland, D. S., & Shanahan, T. (2004). Laying the groundwork for literacy. *Educational Leadership*, 61(6), 74–77.

Taylor, D. B. (2012). Multiliteracies: Moving from theory to practice in teacher education courses. In D. Polly, C. Mims, & K. A. Persichitte (Eds.), *Developing technology-rich teacher education programs: Key issues* (pp. 266–287). Hershey, PA: Information Science Reference.

Taylor, D. B., Mraz, M., Nichols, W. D., Rickelman, R. J., & Wood, K. D. (2009). Using explicit instruction to promote vocabulary learning for struggling readers. *Reading and Writing Quarterly*, *25*(2–3), 205–220.

Thompson, E. (1958). The "master word" approach to vocabulary training. *Journal of Developmental Reading*, *2*(1), 62–66.

Tompkins, G. E. (2010). *Literacy for the 21st century: A balanced approach* (5th ed.). Boston: Allyn & Bacon.

Turner, S. V., & Dipinto, V. M. (1992). Students as hypermedia authors: Themes emerging from a qualitative study. *Journal of Research on Computing in Education*, *25*(2), 187–199.

U.S. Department of Education, Office of Educational Technology. (2010). *Transforming American education: Learning—Powered by technology: National educational technology plan 2010: Executive summary*. Washington, DC: Author. Accessed at http://tech.ed.gov/netp/netp-executive-summary on January 23, 2016.

Vincent, J. (2007). Writing and coding: Assisting writers to cross the modes. *Language and Education*, *21*(2), 141–157.

Visser, R. D., & Evering, L. C. (2013). Using digital tools to enhance literacy. *Reading Matters*, *13*, 32–38.

Vygotsky, L. S. (1978). *Mind in society: The development of higher psychological processes* (M. Cole, V. John-Steiner, S. Scribner, & E. Souberman, Eds.). Cambridge, MA: Harvard University Press.

Warner, G. (1989). *The boxcar children*. Morton Grove, IL: Whitman.

wikiHow. (n.d.). *How to create a book with Book Creator*. Accessed at www.wikihow.com/Create-a-Book-with-Book-Creator on March 21, 2016.

Wolsey, T. D. (2004). Literature discussions in cyberspace: Young adolescents using threaded discussion groups to talk about reading. *Reading Online*, *7*(4). Accessed at www.readingonline.org/articles/art_index.asp?href=wolsey/index.html on August 25, 2015.

Wood, K. D., Roser, N. L., & Martinez, M. (2001). Collaborative literacy: Lessons learned from literature. *The Reading Teacher*, *55*(2), 102–111.

Yearta, L. S. (2012). *The effect of digital word study on fifth graders' vocabulary acquisition, retention, and motivation: A mixed methods approach* (Doctoral dissertation). Accessed at ProQuest dissertations and theses database. (Accession no. 3551954)

Yearta, L. S., & Stover, K. (2015). Beyond the classroom walls: Blogging to increase literacy engagement. *Reading Matters*, *15*, 35–37.

Yearta, L. S., & Wash, P. D. (2015). Digital vocabulary: Greek and Latin root study in the 21st century. *Georgia Journal of Reading*, *38*(2), 24–28.

Young, C., & Rasinski, T. V. (2009). Implementing Readers Theatre as an approach to classroom fluency instruction. *The Reading Teacher*, *63*(1), 4–13.

Young, C., & Stover, K. (2013/2014). "Look what I did!": Student conferences with text-to-speech software. *The Reading Teacher*, *67*(4), 269–272.

zakimi76. (2014, March 25). *Book Creator app tutorial* [Video file]. Accessed at www.youtube .com/watch?v=zP_z-Pvfft8 on March 21, 2016.

Zawilinski, L. (2009). HOT blogging: A framework for blogging to promote higher order thinking. *The Reading Teacher*, *62*(8), 650–661.

Zhang, S., Duke, N. K., & Jiménez, L. M. (2011). The WWWDOT approach to improving students' critical evaluation of websites. *The Reading Teacher*, *65*(2), 150–158.

Zutell, J. (2008). Changing perspectives on word knowledge: Spelling and vocabulary. In M. J. Fresch (Ed.), *An essential history of current reading practices* (pp. 186–206). Newark, DE: International Reading Association.

Index

The Right to Be Literate
Brian M. Pete and Robin J. Fogarty
Explore the six comprehensive skill areas essential to 21st century literacy—reading, writing, listening, speaking, viewing, and representing. Learn practical strategies for teaching students the skills they need to think critically and communicate collaboratively in the digital age.
BKF643

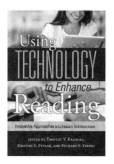

Using Technology to Enhance Reading
Edited by Timothy V. Rasinski, Kristine E. Pytash, and Richard E. Ferdig
Discover how technological resources can improve the effectiveness and breadth of reading instruction to build student knowledge. Read real-world accounts from literacy experts, and learn how their methods can be adapted for your classroom.
BKF608

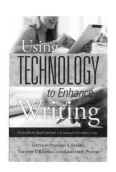

Using Technology to Enhance Writing
Edited by Richard E. Ferdig, Timothy V. Rasinski, and Kristine E. Pytash
Sharpen your students' communication skills while integrating digital tools into writing instruction. Loaded with techniques for planning and organizing writing, this handbook troubleshoots issues students face when writing in a printed versus digital context and teaches them how to read in multiple media.
BKF607

Literacy 2.0
Nancy Frey, Douglas Fisher, and Alex Gonzalez
Students in the 21st century must incorporate traditional literacy skills into a mastery of technology for communicating and collaborating in new ways. This book offers specific teaching strategies for developing students' skills related to acquiring, producing, and sharing information.
BKF373

Wait! Your professional development journey doesn't have to end with the last pages of this book.

We realize improving student learning doesn't happen overnight. And your school or district shouldn't be left to puzzle out all the details of this process alone.

No matter where you are on the journey, we're committed to helping you get to the next stage.

Take advantage of everything from **custom workshops** to **keynote presentations** and **interactive web and video conferencing**. We can even help you develop an action plan tailored to fit your specific needs.

Let's get the conversation started.

Call 888.763.9045 today.

solution-tree.com